What Your Colleagues
Are Saying . . .

"The daily decisions of school leaders are shaped by a set of personal and professional ethics that influence every interaction we have with students, colleagues, and families. Toni Faddis provides clear and coherent guidelines for helping leaders locate and adhere to a set of ethical standards, and interrogate one's own biases. The outcome is an assurance that all decisions, large and small, are grounded in an ethical frame."

Nancy Frey
San Diego State University
Author of *Developing Assessment-Capable Learners*, *Visible Learning for Literacy*,
and many other Corwin books

"An innovative and thoughtful approach to addressing real-life ethical concerns of educational practitioners. With its 10 leadership strategies, *The Ethical Line* is a must-read for all educators. Kudos to Dr. Faddis for this important contribution to the field."

Jacqueline Stefkovich, JD
Professor Emerita, The Pennsylvania State University
Author of *Multiple Ethical Paradigms*

"Dr. Faddis skillfully captures the very essence of what leaders at all levels of the organization must do to solve complex issues in which there are no easy solutions. In a time where integrity and ethical leadership is paramount when faced with solving tough issues, Dr. Faddis provides hope and proven strategies to keep leaders from crossing the ethical line."

David Lorden
Former District Superintendent

"I have come to know and rely on Toni Faddis as an effective equity-driven school leader. I have every confidence that those who read this book will come to the same conclusion. More importantly, the book presents 10 ethically driven strategies to help us become the school leaders that our children, families, educators, and communities deserve."

Ian Pumpian
Professor of Educational Leadership, San Diego State University
Author of *How to Create a Culture of Achievement in Your School and Classroom*
and *Building Equity: Policies and Practices to Empower All Learners*

"Toni Faddis provides a vital work for our time. Schooling is not less complex, it is more complex by the day. In *The Ethical Line*, we are reminded that schools are 'people places' and only ethical leaders can build the kind of community necessary for each student to thrive and communities to reach their full potential together."

Bradley Portin
Professor and Dean Emeritus, University of Washington–Bothell

"In today's diverse educational systems, leading through an ethical lens is more important than ever. In *The Ethical Line*, Dr. Faddis presents thoughtful, practical strategies for navigating the moral and ethical challenges educators face each day."

Janice Cook
Former Superintendent

"As an administrator, being able to have a tool that supports the conversation around ethics makes a strong impact on our school culture. This book allows everyone in the school setting to have common language and understanding of what an ethical school looks and feels like. This book supports the growth of any leader and school community when dealing with difficult situations."

Dominique Smith
Author of *Building Equity: Policies and Practices to Empower All Learners* and *Carrots Are Better Than Sticks*

"Today's leadership preparation programs aim to create leaders who strive to take personal responsibility for providing the environment that produce empowered, engaged, inspired, and successful learners. In thinking about principal preparation programs, *The Ethical Line* is the reading that will push your candidates to achieve just this by thinking deeply and reflecting upon who they are and what type of leader they will be once they enter the ranks of school leadership. Dr. Faddis's easy-to-read, practitioner-friendly text provides activities that enhance classroom discussion and complement any program committed to equity-driven leadership and ethical decision making. I highly recommend integrating this important book into your program."

Lori Rhodes
Assistant Professor, California State University, Sonoma

"Dr. Faddis has written an exemplar piece to support and guide school leaders in developing and utilizing an ethical lens when leading diverse schools. *The Ethical Line* illustrates the need for ethical leadership in a way that is conceivable and achievable, through the implementation of 10 key strategies. This is an essential read for all current and future PreK–12 leaders."

Sarah Graham
Assistant Professor, California State University, Sacramento

THE ETHICAL LINE

THE ETHICAL LINE

10 Leadership Strategies for Effective Decision Making

Toni Faddis

Foreword by Douglas Fisher

FOR INFORMATION:

Corwin

A SAGE Company

2455 Teller Road

Thousand Oaks, California 91320

(800) 233-9936

www.corwin.com

SAGE Publications Ltd.

1 Oliver's Yard

55 City Road

London EC1Y 1SP

United Kingdom

SAGE Publications India Pvt. Ltd.

B 1/I 1 Mohan Cooperative Industrial Area

Mathura Road, New Delhi 110 044

India

SAGE Publications Asia-Pacific Pte. Ltd.

18 Cross Street #10-10/11/12

China Square Central

Singapore 048423

Printed in the United States of America

Library of Congress Cataloging-in-Publication Data

Names: Faddis, Toni, author.

Title: The ethical line : 10 leadership strategies for effective decision making / Toni Faddis.

Description: Thousand Oaks, California : Corwin, [2020] | Includes bibliographical references and index.

Identifiers: LCCN 2019006739 | ISBN 9781544337883 (pbk. : alk. paper)

Subjects: LCSH: Educational leadership—Moral and ethical aspects. | Educational leadership—Decision making.

Classification: LCC LB2806 .F34 2020 | DDC 371.2/011—dc23

LC record available at https://lccn.loc.gov/2019006739

This book is printed on acid-free paper.

Publisher: Arnis Burvikovs

Development Editor: Desirée A. Bartlett

Senior Editorial Assistant: Eliza B. Erickson

Production Editor: Tori Mirsadjadi

Copy Editor: Terri Lee Paulsen

Typesetter: C&M Digitals (P) Ltd.

Proofreader: Victoria Reed-Castro

Indexer: Terri Morrissey

Cover and Interior Designer: Candice Harman

Marketing Manager: Sharon Pendergast

Certified Chain of Custody
Promoting Sustainable Forestry
www.sfiprogram.org
SFI-01268

SFI label applies to text stock

19 20 21 22 23 10 9 8 7 6 5 4 3 2 1

CONTENTS

FOREWORD

I remember my ethics class from undergraduate school. *Boring*. It was all theories, and most of them from a long time ago. We read, and were tested on, ideas such as Relativism, Utilitarianism, and Deontology. The highlight of the course was the ethical debate. We were randomly assigned debate topics and I got animal rights. I was assigned to read *Animal Liberation* (Singer, 1975), which was a good book but I was not able to make the connection between the theories much less with my work as a future teacher. I passed the class (mostly because of my debate score) and did not think much about ethics, or moral decision making, for several years.

Little did I know how much ethics would come into play in my professional life. Ethics, as the *Internet Encyclopedia of Philosophy* tells us, "involves systematizing, defending, and recommending concepts of right and wrong behavior" (www.iep.utm.edu/ethics). The field of ethics is generally divided into three subcategories:

- Metaethics, which focuses on the origin of ethical principles and what those principals generally mean.
- Normative ethics, which focuses on moral standards that suggest right and wrong conduct.
- Applied ethics, which requires the examination of specific controversial issues within an ethical framework.

My undergraduate class was focused mainly on metaethics with an applied ethics task. As an early professional, I was looking for more information about expectations for conduct and the ways in which I could challenge the norm of schooling while not crossing a line that would suggest unethical behavior. I needed to understand my moral compass as well as the non-negotiable standards in my profession so that I could walk the line, pushing forward without violating the moral code of my profession.

I now realize that there is nothing wrong with learning about meta-ethics, but professionals also need normative and applied ethics. As Toni Faddis notes, leaders' days are filled with ethical decisions and leaders must be aware of their Ethical Line as well as the impact of each of their decisions. They need to understand normative ethics and how those guidelines are applied in practice. And, they need to know how to advocate for students and changes to the system without getting fired for unethical actions. As she suggests, "Ethics is at the heart of good leadership." I could not agree more. People look to their leaders to make decisions that are fair, just, and reasonable. These people include students, teachers, staff, parents, community members, district office leaders, and many others. It's a heavy burden to be faced with an ethical dilemma and know that you must make an informed decision that conforms with the standard of care expected in your community.

Thankfully, *The Ethical Line* provides case studies and strategies that leaders can use to make these decisions. I appreciate that this resource starts with getting to know your own moral core values. We all operate from these values and must check them for bias, which Toni helps us do in the first section. I also appreciate the section on legal parameters. The examples and ideas in this book operationalize the professional standards for educational leaders and provide concrete tools that we can all use when we need to make a decision.

Some decisions are easy. That's not what this book is about. This book is about those hard decisions—the decisions that we ponder and reflect on way into the night. This book is about building a habit of making decisions that serve our profession, and the students who need us, well. And it's about developing a professional dialogue about the role of ethics in leadership. I invite you to join the conversation, knowing that you will be a stronger leader as a result of engaging in this type of ethics learning.

—*Douglas Fisher*

REFERENCE

Singer, P. (1975). *Animal liberation: A new ethics for our treatment of animals.* New York: Random House.

ACKNOWLEDGMENTS

I am incredibly grateful for the support I received while developing the concept of The Ethical Line, which eventually led to this book. First and foremost, I wish to thank my husband, Jimmy, for being my rock: his unyielding encouragement and support helped me to overcome the challenges associated with putting my thoughts on paper. I would like to acknowledge my parents, Joe and Judy Osborn, because they instilled a strong work ethic in me from a young age and shared practical wisdom accumulated over a lifetime of service to students and families. I wish to thank Antwon Lincoln for being a thought partner in the early stages of this endeavor; his enthusiasm confirmed my belief that ethical decision making is a relevant and interesting topic for school leaders. I am very grateful to Doug Fisher for having faith in me and for believing that I have something to say.

I have benefited greatly from my experiences in school systems, particularly the partnerships that were founded on kindness and trust. I would like to thank Olivia Amador, my kindred spirit who always has my back. I am grateful to David Lorden, who has become a mentor and good friend to me. I am also thankful to the countless students, teachers, and community members who trusted me and worked with me to plan and execute actions that effected positive change in our corner of the world.

Finally, I am indebted to the Corwin family, especially Arnis Burvikovs, Desirée Bartlett, and Eliza Erickson, for your assistance throughout this project. Your feedback and guidance were invaluable, and I thank you for this opportunity.

PUBLISHER'S ACKNOWLEDGMENTS

Corwin gratefully acknowledges the contributions of the following reviewers:

Ray Boyd
Principal
Beechboro, Western Australia

Virginia E. Kelsen
Executive Director, Career Readiness
Ontario, CA

Holly Leach
Superintendent
Everett, WA

Jacie Maslyk
Assistant Superintendent, Author
Coraopolis, PA

Nancy M. Moga
Principal
Covington, VA

Angela M. Mosley
Principal
Henrico, VA

Cynthia Pilar
Project Lead, California Principals' Support Network
University of California, Davis

Leslie Standerfer
Principal
Goodyear, AZ

ABOUT THE AUTHOR

Dr. Toni Faddis has served as a public school educator for the past 25 years as a teacher, principal, and district leader. She is also a faculty member of the Educational Leadership Department at San Diego State University, teaching a course on ethical leadership, problem-solving, and communication skills to teachers who aspire to become school principals.

Toni has a wealth of experience and knowledge as a learning leader. For 13 years she was principal of two schools close to the United States–Mexico border and established strong, collaborative teacher teams that resulted in improved content delivery, greater student achievement, and increased teacher self-efficacy. As a district leader, Toni coaches and supports aspiring, novice, and veteran administrators.

Toni's passion for educational excellence, equity, and ethical school leadership led to doctoral research regarding principal decision making in border school communities. The degree, conferred by San Diego State University, marked the end of Toni's study, but not of her learning journey. Toni looks for something new to learn every day and is committed to improving access and outcomes for learners of all ages.

Toni can be reached at tonifaddis.com.

INTRODUCTION

When I was a new principal, at the end of each day I could usually be found puzzling over that day's dilemma. Looking back, I'm sure there wasn't a dilemma every single day, but at the time it seemed like it. Besides being challenged by the people-centered situations that occur on every school campus, I also felt inundated with a tsunami of tasks, meetings, and community members who all wanted to talk to me. As a teacher, I was in control of my schedule and had the ability to decompress after students had left at the end of the day. As a principal, I quickly learned that "before school" and "afterschool" was not downtime to complete the compliance-oriented functions of my job that needed to be done. Those hours were filled with conversations with parents, staff members, and students and were frequently related to that day's dilemma.

Because of the weight of the dilemmas (those situations always felt "heavy" to me), I felt that the process of making a sound decision was as essential as the outcome. Making personal connections to truly understand all aspects of an issue through deliberate questioning and careful listening is essential to get to the heart of the matter. These efforts signaled to others that I valued them and the situation at hand. Sending an e-mail was a last resort if I wasn't able to make contact with someone. Even people who do not agree with your decisions appreciate when the principal is visible, accessible, and transparent with decision-making processes. I found these "touchpoints" to be vital to my success as a principal.

These touchpoints—authentically connecting, listening, and collaborating with people—became hallmarks of my leadership style. I quickly learned to seek people out before they came looking for me. I began to prepare for meetings days in advance so that I would always be available and present for the day's events. I had my fair share of dilemmas as a new principal; although some felt lighter than others, all were extremely heavy to those involved.

Over the past 13 years as a school principal, I have studied the actions of a range of educators, some highly effective, and others less skilled. These observations, coupled with my introspective nature, have allowed me to hone particular strategies to effectively manage diverse school communities and foster student achievement. Because of the demanding nature of the principalship, I also employed practices to relax and reenergize; these routines helped me to decompress and manage all of the administrative tasks while actualizing an educational vision for students. I explain these self-care strategies by detailing each in relation to school leadership.

This leadership framework puts you in the driver's seat. It is flexible in that you are able to align it to your own core values. When this alignment exists, you feel balanced and in control—both personally and professionally. Being an effective leader in today's diverse school communities is not easy, nor is it simple. The field of education has changed drastically in the 21st century, making the work of educating students significantly more challenging. Education policies and standards have changed, teaching practices have changed, and the students we serve have changed. To be the leaders our society needs us to be, instructional pedagogy and operational expertise are necessary but are not enough; it is through skillful interactions, collaboration, and reflective leadership that we will achieve our school missions.

THE ETHICAL LINE

When I first started thinking about the ethical behavior of school leaders, I imagined a line on the ground that divided ethical actions from unethical actions. I came to understand that each of us has our own ethical line. Our ethical line is our moral compass—the voice in our head that guides our thoughts and actions. The way I see it, as we go about our typical day all of us walk atop of our ethical lines. Stepping off the line for the right reason doesn't make you an unethical person. Educators actually need to step off the line sometimes to make decisions that are in the best interest of students. We need to do this because there isn't always a rule or policy that applies to a given situation or following the policy would actually be a disservice to the child in question. In one sense, we step off of our line when we choose not to adhere to a policy. On the other hand, we also are true to our ethical line if we do this to act in the best interest of a child or group of children. As our leadership skills develop, we become aware of the many situations that don't have easy answers. The "right" or "ethical" answer isn't always simple or apparent. Decision making depends quite a lot on context and consequences. Our decision-making patterns in wealthy, private schools will likely look different from the decisions we make when we are serving in struggling communities. The needs are different, so our considerations and priorities also need to be different. When we change contexts or consider situations from a different point of view, we might find that our ethical line shifts slightly. To ensure that we continue to act ethically and in the best interests of our students, it's critical that we continually practice self-reflection to check to see if we're making decisions for the right reasons.

Our actions, both conscious and unconscious, are influenced by our values, habits, cultural orientations, and past experiences. These aspects of character also drive the ways in which we approach dilemmas, essentially establishing our own personal ethical line. Given the wide range of issues and pressures that school leaders face, chances are we will make some mistakes along the way. We will make errors in judgment. We are not perfect; no one is. Nonetheless, it is our responsibility to maintain our ethical line, to lead by example, and to help others to work through issues when conflicts arise.

Our integrity will be most in demand during times of conflict. Times of conflict are challenging and demanding, but they are also opportunities for growth and development. By paying attention to the challenges we face now, we will be able to improve our future behaviors and decisions. Furthermore, defining moments (discussed in Strategy #10) reveal opportunities to learn from others, as well as guide other people. We must remind ourselves that dilemmas are made more complex because of the conflicting needs of the people involved. When we find ourselves in such situations, it is important that we examine our biases and instincts, making an effort to view the dilemma from multiple angles and multiple points of view. As leaders we often feel the need to satisfy people who have a wide range of values, interests, and agendas. Making decisions during these trying times further cements our character, both as a moment of our own personal growth and how others perceive who we are and what we stand for. More often than not, we have to accept the fact that we will have to disappoint some people in order to move forward toward the ultimate goal of serving students' best interests.

As I reflect upon the past 13 years as a school leader, I am reminded of a line from one of Emily Dickinson's letters to a friend (Higginson, 1891): "The sailor cannot see the North, but knows the needle can." Whenever I felt overcome in a sea of complex challenges and competing interests, I learned to trust my moral compass to guide me. Attentively adhering to this ethical line has helped me proceed with confidence and peace of mind. Pausing for self-reflection allows my core beliefs and values to shape my behavior. Acting upon your core beliefs is critical to successfully and effectively leading in a manner that is consistent, purposeful, and ethical.

TEMPTATIONS LURK EVERYWHERE

People generally expect those in the public eye to behave ethically, although glaring exceptions from Wells Fargo, Volkswagen, Uber, and The Weinstein Company all suggest these organizations have struggled with internal integrity issues and ethical decision making. Scandals involving school administrators cheating on high-stakes tests, having affairs with students, and accounts of financial mismanagement prove that educators are not immune to moral failings.

People are human; we struggle to make good choices all the time. We are continually tempted to overeat, stay up too late, and to veer from a preplanned budget. While these personal behaviors may be trivial, cutting corners professionally can lead to significant negative consequences. Therefore, as educators who have been entrusted with the community's most prized treasure—their children—we must take steps to adhere to a high ethical standard. For as Nancy Tuana, an American philosopher and director of the Rock Ethics Institute at Penn State, has said, ethical proficiency is a "lifelong achievement, for we find ourselves confronted with new, and sometimes unique, ethical issues throughout our lifetimes" (Tuana, 2014, p. 154). Ethical leadership is not likely to happen unintentionally or by instinct. Sadly, most of us have had little to no formal training in ethics or in the nature of ethical decision making. Therefore, it is my hope that this book can offer structured guidance on how to pause and reflect on your own personal values and commitments as well as some tools and strategies for applying rigorous ethical thoughtfulness to complex decisions. The goal is to be prepared ahead of time. Chances are that sometime in the near future you will be faced with temptations—to ignore injustice, to take the easy path, to make decisions in isolation, to not put in the time and effort to consider the consequences of potential decisions. When those temptations arise, it is my hope that you will already have at your fingertips effective tools to tackle ethical dilemmas responsibly and ethically.

TOUGH CHOICES

Education leaders are forced to make tough choices. Tough choices don't always involve criminal laws, codes of conduct, or headline-worthy issues. Sometimes the struggle involves our tightly held core values being in conflict with one another. Tough choices are typically the ones that pit one "right" value against another "right" value. Consider this dilemma: A student confesses that he accidentally brought a Swiss Army knife to school this morning. He had it in his backpack when he went to a Scouts meeting last night. He tells you that he thought he had removed it, but he must have forgotten. "Are you going to suspend me?" he asks, with tears in his eyes. This student is at the top of the class and has never been in trouble. Your inclination is to make this a teachable moment, but there is a zero-tolerance policy for weapons at the school. What do you do? During cases of right versus wrong, there is usually a clear path of action to take, thus allowing us to make a good decision, and move on. The really tough choices, then, don't focus on right versus wrong. They involve right versus right decisions, or ethical dilemmas. These are genuine dilemmas because each side is deeply rooted in one of our core values. In this case, we value the right of this child to an education (i.e., not being suspended), but we also value upholding a strong practice of security and a practice where no one receives special treatment. Which is the most ethical decision?

Other ethical dilemmas might arise such as: What does employee discipline look like after a child is injured during the short period of time when an ailing teacher left her students unsupervised? How should you proceed when two middle school teachers begin a visible romance on your campus? What should be done when a white teacher disciplines an energetic black student by sending her to another class because the teacher "needs a break"? These dilemmas are both routine and extremely challenging. They require solid judgment to make a worthy resolution. Rarely do educators receive any training in thinking through complex situations to arrive at responses that are fair, legal, and in the best interests of students. These problems are ethical challenges of equity, inclusion, fairness, and human rights.

HOW THIS BOOK CAN HELP

This book is your guide to successfully navigating the complex circumstances that school leaders face in today's complex and diverse societies. Training in reflection, ethical action, and how to avoid decision-making traps are crucial to one's personal well-being, professional character, and to the treatment and opportunities offered to our students. The goal of this book is to provide structured opportunities for you to reflect on your own values and leadership practices while offering strategies and decision-making processes that rest on a foundation of ethical behaviors.

By considering your own values, beliefs, and biases now, in the future you will:

- Have confidence that you have the skills to expose the ethical considerations and implications of problems faced by leaders in diverse environments
- Be certain that your decision-making processes are sound and improve educational outcomes for students
- Feel empowered to do right by students, while reducing or eliminating harmful practices that marginalize groups of students

FEATURES YOU WILL FIND

- 10 strategies that can be applied to prevent or overcome future problematic situations
- 10 true case-study examples from current educators that readers can use to examine the ethical aspects of common issues facing school leaders
- Activities in each chapter that encourage you to apply the lessons of the chapter to your own context
- Reflective questions in each chapter prompting you to consider your own values while weighing the various aspects of an ethical dilemma to help shape your future leadership actions
- A discussion of Professional Standards for Educational Leaders (PSEL) Standard 2: *Ethics and Professional Norms* and Standard 3: *Equity and Cultural Responsiveness* so that you are better informed of your obligations to students
- Tools that foster collaborative leadership by enlisting the cooperation of staff and community members

Effectively and ethically leading schools through the new and unique demands of today's world begins in our schools and requires leaders who have a vision that ensures all groups of students not only learn but feel welcomed, supported, and valued—not in spite of their differences but because of them. This type of leadership requires courage and an ability to collaborate with others, because it's not possible for one person, no matter how effective or ethical, to nourish and sustain a community alone. While this responsibility is shared, it starts at the top. The principal's commitment to ethical and inclusive practices must permeate the school community at all levels—to staff, families, and students—such that each individual considers himself or herself to be an ethical leader.

I constantly and consciously seek to balance my personal beliefs with those of my school community. I am fully aware that my upbringing as a Caucasian female has afforded me certain privileges that have shaped the person I am today. I must regularly ask myself: *What am I trying to achieve? Which values am I signaling, both intentionally and unintentionally, to my students and my school community?* I would like to believe that my actions are sincere efforts to be culturally responsive to my students, school community, and my organization. I strive to maintain a culture of feedback such that I can understand my impact. To maintain my ethical line, I depend on these 10 strategies:

Strategies for Successful and Ethical Leadership

Strategy #1: Identify and Model Your Core Values

Strategy #2: Be Curiously Introspective

Strategy #3: Listen Generously

Strategy #4: Create an Inclusive School Climate

Strategy #5: Discover Your Community's Hopes and Dreams

Strategy #6: Unify Around a Collective Vision

Strategy #7: Consider Moral and Legal Consequences of Decisions

Strategy #8: Ensure Equitable Processes and Outcomes

Strategy #9: Walk the Talk

Strategy #10: Become a Strategic Influencer

Ethics is at the heart of good leadership. Every choice an education leader makes is based upon a particular context and is influenced by her or his experiences, values, and cultural orientations. Each chapter of this book focuses on two to four of these strategies, offering examples, tools, activities, and questions for reflection. The case studies presented in each chapter are derived from diverse contexts. They describe complex dilemmas that should cause you to pause and carefully consider how you might handle the situation for the benefit of all. As you read each case study, I invite you to widen your gaze and shift your perspective to consider all angles of the situation and the perspective of each key figure. These case studies are an opportunity for you to imagine expanding your metacognitive and leadership skills while nurturing the health and well-being of your school community. It is my dream that ultimately every child in your care will benefit because you took the tenets in this book to heart. I hope this book will help you consciously identify your core values, so that you can lead always staying true to your own ethical line.

KNOW THYSELF

From college deans to middle school principals to preschool directors, school administrators are responsible for instructional, financial, and equitable leadership while ensuring the steady day-to-day operational management of our educational organizations. What guides your decisions as a leader? Chances are your decisions are guided by a combination of your personal code of ethics, family values, prior experience, and the policies and laws governing your profession, your district, and your school. All of these factors go into forming and defining your Ethical Line.

Reflective Questions

■ Has there been a time in your career when you felt conflicted because your personal values clashed with the professional norms of your school or district? How did you handle the dilemma of adhering to your own Ethical Line vs. following the norms and regulations of your organization?

■ How did you feel after having moved ahead with your decision?

■ Have there been times when you have actively challenged a rule because you believed it was flawed? What happened as a result?

■ When might you take such a risk?

■ What are you willing to stand up for?

■ If you decide to take a stand, how do you judge whether or not you're right?

Without careful self-examination and reflection about personal values and beliefs, leaders run the risk of making a questionable decision that puts them and the organization in professional peril. This chapter begins with the self. Here you will find two strategies to help you access your options when moral dilemmas arise. Strategy #1 will help you identify and reflect on your core values and leadership style. Strategy #2 offers specific ways to unpack the uncomfortable emotions that accompany problems, learn from them, and move on. Consciously leading with your core values and eliminating unnecessary mental chatter will bolster your resolve, facilitating your ability to lead ethically and confidently.

STRATEGY #1: IDENTIFY AND MODEL YOUR CORE VALUES

THE NEW NORMAL

The role of the school principal has changed dramatically in recent years (Hull, 2018). Whereas in previous eras the principal was responsible for building administration and operational duties, today's principals are expected to be instructional leaders, culture builders, and data analyzers who guide school improvement efforts as well as manage building operations (Alvoid & Black, 2014). Student achievement data, once difficult for citizens to locate, is now easily found with a quick Internet search. As a result, the public is more involved in school functions, has more informed opinions, and has greater expectations of the school system and principals.

When you think of a principal from your own personal school experience, what images come to mind? Some people cite that the principal was a disciplinarian who ruled an iron fist. Others clearly remember the use of corporal punishment by their principal while others say they only remember the principal because his or her picture appeared on the class composite from the local photography company. Though we have different memories of that person, most of us will agree that it seemed like the principal was a permanent fixture at the school, often serving 10 to 20 years in the same office. Nowadays, the notion that the principal is permanent no longer holds true. Results from the 2016–2017 school year indicate that nearly 20% of public school principals changed schools or left the profession. These statistics have remained constant since 2008 (National Center for Educational Statistics [NCES], 2018c).

Principals face more scrutiny from the public than ever before. Society is concerned with the state of public education and how well our students perform in math when compared to students in other countries. The community wants to know how money is allocated to different programs and if their kid will go to Sea World this year. Parent involvement used to mean supporting school activities through bake sales. The National Education Association (NEA) reports that many states now require that education policy includes parents as decision makers in matters of school business. People are more actively involved in their children's education than ever before (NEA, 2012).

Under the watchful eyes of the public, principals are also confronted by changing demographics in their schools. Increasing diversity, including racial, ethnic, linguistic, LGBTQ groups, and growing numbers of students with disabilities, have surfaced new challenges in school settings. Principals are tasked with ensuring the wide range of academic, emotional, and social needs of students are being met. Peter DeWitt's (2017) top 10 list of critical issues that principals face on a daily basis includes the school-to-prison pipeline, student learning, social media, and the effects of poverty. A 2012 survey by MetLife indicated that principals feel their job responsibilities are remarkably different from just five years before, and 75% of those reported that their jobs are too complex and have led to higher degrees of stress and decreased job satisfaction (MetLife, 2012). Changing expectations, coupled with inadequate training and support, have led many principals to conclude that their jobs are no longer sustainable (Alvoid & Black, 2014).

Ten years ago, social media was not a *thing*. Today it is a *thing* and we are acutely aware of public posts to Facebook, Twitter, and other platforms. We are concerned that students use social media and instant messaging to communicate rapidly with their peers. We are worried about their quick access to cameras and video recorders. We are distressed that students are able to circulate inappropriate pictures and are quick to press the record button to film themselves and others. While technology has certainly played a positive role in transforming education, other aspects have led to disastrous consequences for the victims of slander, bullying, and other character smears. Each of these issues represent ethical challenges for principals.

Principals also grapple with local, state, and national policies that may be at odds with each other (Hull, 2018). For example, in recent years there has been a shift in some communities toward a restorative approach instead of punishment when a student misbehaves. The Obama administration was concerned with disparate suspension rates between African American students and other groups, taking steps to rectify unfair disciplinary practices. The Trump administration is taking a different approach, disregarding restorative practices but providing guidelines for schools who choose to arm their teachers (Meckler, 2018). Principals who choose to take the restorative approach find themselves needing to justify their decisions to parents who demand punishment for the perpetrator when their child is the victim or teachers who insist stringent consequences and high standards are in the best interest of the students.

Because of the evolving and complex nature of the job, being a school principal is no easy feat. The leadership terrain is often muddled by obstructions and hurdles that may require us to think fast, reevaluate, and make necessary pivots. Plans fail, people move, and there seems to be never-ending budget cuts that require leaders to stretch dollars further and further.

While principals from previous eras had power to rule unilaterally from their offices, today's leaders are expected to work collaboratively, involving others in decision making. They are facilitators who help others to understand policy and context while ensuring discussions are inclusive. A chief role of the principal is to assist groups of people with divergent interests to come to a consensus in service of student learning. Today's principals are unable to rely on a one-size-fits-all method that may have worked with a past generation; instead, they must be innovative problem solvers.

Further, solving problems is unlike previous eras when the principal could impose a decision or rule without rebuke. Today's principals must consider how local and national policies might impact a wide range of diverse community members, who may have their own competing interests (see Figure 1.1). These problems, some of which feel unsurmountable, combined with a nonstop pace have resulted in high

Figure 1.1   Characteristics of Public Schools: Then and Now

The Previous Generation	Today's Realities
Education as a profession was steady.	The principal hand delivers lay-off notices to teachers each year.
Principals managed school operations.	Principals manage school operations and are the instructional leaders on campus.
Principals suspended the rowdy kids.	Principals respect the rights of students and do not deny education because of poor behavioral choices. Principals coax, entice, and reward children for being in class.
Parents respected school personnel and supported their decisions.	Parents insist that their children are "innocent" and would "never lie." Principals must bear the burden of proof to parents.
Students ate breakfast at home before school.	Seventy percent of students in U.S. public schools are eligible for free or reduced-price lunch. (NCES, 2018b)

levels of principal turnover, especially in lower socioeconomic neighborhoods (Branch, Hanushek, & Rivkin, 2013).

Our understanding of ourselves and our profession should continue to deepen and grow throughout our lifetimes. Successful leaders keep up to date by continually reading and discussing emerging educational research as well as by staying current with what's in the news. Regular attendance at workshops and conferences are opportunities to learn, build networks, and grow content knowledge. By taking advantage of these learning opportunities, you will extend your understanding of educational practices, are more likely to anticipate potential barriers that may pop up, and are better equipped to make sense of sensitive situations that arise at your school site.

Today's realities in schools necessitate that principals are prepared to have conversations with students, staff, and parents that were unlikely only a few years ago. Current topics such as gender-neutral bathrooms, transgender teens who play on boys' and girls' sports teams, and beliefs about prayers during the school day are often highly sensitive and may result in ethical dilemmas because of people's views. "Because ethical dilemmas are so value laden, it is essential that school leaders understand their own values and value positions" (Cranston, Ehrich, & Kimber, 2014, p. 240). As such, we must be able to articulate, and defend if necessary, what we truly stand for.

> "Because ethical dilemmas are so value laden, it is essential that school leaders understand their own values and value positions" (Cranston, Ehrich, & Kimber, 2014, p. 240).

Commitment to our ideals is what makes us ethical leaders. This unwavering devotion establishes a reputation as a leader, parent, community member, or employee. It is a conscious effort to be explicit about what you believe in and what you're not willing to let go. Consistently leading with our core values is one way to earn respect from others in the organization and school community. People take cues from the ways in which the leader behaves. As people get to know you, they come to expect how you will respond in given situations.

Strategies, goals, and missions may change; however, values are your core and remain intact despite new conditions, new laws, and new goals (Starr, 2016). Certainly, there are open and shut cases that do not require strategic thinking and careful analysis of solutions. Some issues can be handled by adhering to a policy or maintaining a child-centered approach. Often, we are able to resolve these "no brainers" because we have a firm understanding and devotion to our core values. So, what do you believe in? Why do you feel that way? How do your beliefs influence your actions?

ACTIVITY 1.1

Identify Your Core Values

As a leader, it is important that you be able to succinctly articulate your leadership values, such that you are able to speak of them easily, infuse them into professional conversations, and lead based upon that awareness. A manager of an environmentally focused nonprofit may identify her core values as the environment, service, and creativity. A police officer may state that security, control, and integrity are the backbone of his work. It is important to be conscious of what our own personal values (see Figure 1.2) are so that we can evaluate whether the decisions we make match up to the values we have articulated.

Step 1. Reflect

Consider the values listed on the next page in relation to your career, not your personal life.

Step 2. Identify

Circle five values that you consider to be cornerstones of your leadership. Which values elicit strong feelings within you? Which can you not imagine leading without? Choose five, or feel free to include additional values that are not listed in Figure 1.2

(Continued)

(Continued)

Figure 1.2   List of Core Values

Achievement	Fairness	Loyalty
Adventure	Family	Morality
Affection	Flexibility	Order
Awareness	Freedom	Power
Balance	Friendship	Predictability
Challenge	Happiness	Recognition
Collaboration	Hard Work	Reliability
Comfort	Harmony	Respect
Communication	Helpfulness	Responsibility
Compliance	Honesty	Responsiveness
Control	Improvement	Risk
Cooperation	Inclusiveness	Security
Courage	Independence	Self-respect
Creativity	Initiative	Service
Culture	Innovation	Success
Curiosity	Integrity	Support
Directness	Involvement	Tradition
Diversity	Justice	Transparency
Environment	Kindness	Trust
Equity	Learning	Truthfulness
Excellence	Likeability	Valor
Expertise		Variety
		Wisdom

Step 3. Focus

Now that you have identified five values, cross two of them off. This might be challenging, but it's important to truly identify the essence of your leadership. Once you have identified the top three core values that are most important to you, take notice of why these three stood out to you. There is often a reason, story, or a belief that deeply resonates with you. Use the lines below to record your top three core values and the reasons behind them.

Core Value #1: _____   Underlying reason: _____

Core Value #2: _____   Underlying reason: _____

Core Value #3: _____   Underlying reason: _____

Step 4. Communicate

Our beliefs drive our actions. As leaders, it is important to communicate our core values to the community we serve so that they know what we stand for and how decisions have been approached and informed. Now that you have identified your three core values, how might you reference them during discussions, presentations, meetings, e-mails, newsletters, or other communications? When you are transparent with your values and consistently communicate them verbally and nonverbally, people take notice of your character and what you believe in. Abiding by your core values also helps you stay true to yourself. The ability to name your core values, as well as lead in service of them, builds your credibility as a leader in your community.

YOUR ETHICAL LINE

Strategy #1: *Identify and Model Your Core Values* is the first step in understanding, defining, and acknowledging your Ethical Line. Think of your Ethical Line as your moral compass; it is that voice in your head that guides your thoughts and actions; it steers you toward your true north. Our Ethical Line is influenced by our values, temperaments, and our personal experiences.

> Think of your Ethical Line as your moral compass; it is that voice in your head that guides your thoughts and actions; it steers you toward your true north.

To become familiar with your Ethical Line, you might consider

- reflecting on your own micro-ethics: specific behaviors during your interpersonal interactions each day;
- articulating your core beliefs;
- investigating the shared values of your organization; and
- making sense of the relationship between your Ethical Line and the values of your organization.

Our Ethical Line is not fixed; contextual factors influence our decision paths. Throughout a career, our Ethical Lines continue to mold and adjust according to our surroundings, changing priorities, and new information. It is also shaped by the different leaders we encounter, local and state accountability measures, our school communities, and the values of our organization. As you do your due diligence keeping up to date with your profession and the changing times, you will find moments when you are called upon to reevaluate your Ethical Line.

RIGHT VS. RIGHT SITUATIONS

We all face tough decisions. We may find ourselves worrying endlessly over possible outcomes or agonizing about which course of action to take. The root cause of worry and anxiety during the decision-making process is the little voice inside your head that reminds you of your core values. Just as our values vary from those of our colleagues, so too might our personal values conflict within ourselves. Have you ever had this feeling, when one of your values conflicts with another because of the situation at hand? You can see both sides, and you have a hard time choosing. In situations like these, we might feel like we're in the impossible position of choosing between two conflicting "rights."

THE CASE OF RIGHT VS. RIGHT

Principal Stone
Elementary School
North Carolina

An example of a right vs. right situation occurred to an elementary principal (we'll call him George Stone). Principal Stone was informed that a parent was continually violating the kindergarten student drop-off policy. The policy requires a parent to physically walk the child to class each morning, ensuring that the 5-year-old child is never out of sight of the parent or the teacher. Upon investigation, Principal Stone learned that a parent, Ms. Montes, was unable to walk her child, Ramon, to class each morning because her work schedule had recently changed. Since she was required to get to work earlier than before, she had recruited her fifth-grade son, Javier, to walk Ramon to class. Ms. Montes understood and appreciated the policy designed to keep children safe, but she felt her older son was capable of walking Ramon to class. This became a problem when other parents started complaining that they didn't want to be inconvenienced by finding a parking spot to walk their children to class if Ms. Montes didn't have to. Principal Stone understood Ms. Montes' work predicament and wanted to be helpful, but now that other parents were disregarding the policy he began to worry for the children's safety.

> Dilemma: Principal Stone is a reasonable person who cares deeply about the welfare of his students; his dilemma is that he is unable to generate a satisfactory compromise.

> Reflection: What should Principal Stone do? What would you do?

In one recent study of aspiring principals' preparation programs, it was revealed that there is a general lack of formal ethical training in the field of education (Greer, Searby, & Thoma, 2015). Without substantial preparation and training in ethical reasoning, educators are left to struggle with these challenges on their own. These challenges compel us to think very carefully about our own values and moral principles as well as those individuals who are affected by the situation. Many principals wrestle over the decisions that they make, knowing that there can be more than one right answer; sometimes decisions do not have a right vs. wrong option. What might be the "right" solution to one person (Ms. Montes) may not work for others (other frustrated parents).

In the case of Principal Stone, he is caught between two right decisions. From one point of view, he understands Ms. Montes' need to have her older child walk her 5-year-old to class so she can get to work on time. From another point of view, he is committed to student safety by enforcing the school policy of parents personally handing off kindergartners to their teachers. What Principal Stone decides may set a precedent, or it may not. Either way, Principal Stone must be prepared to justify his decision to community members.

Like Principal Stone, as you consider all aspects of a dilemma, it is likely that you will see more than one "right" way to respond. Figure 1.3 presents real-life dilemmas that require you to consider your Ethical Line, teachable moments, and possible decisions. Ultimately, you have to make a choice that could have serious repercussions to children and families. Will you be able to live with your choice?

Figure 1.3 Examples of Dilemmas

Dilemma	Ethical Line	Options
Example 1 Jayden, a 6-year-old, brings a butter knife to school to spread the peanut butter to the edges of the bread on his sandwich because that's what he does at home. There is a "no weapons" policy at the school. There is no stipulation for age or other factors.	Your conscience tells you that there are different approaches you might take when attending to this situation. On the one hand, you take into consideration the importance of implementing the school rule fairly to all students without showing favoritism. On the other hand, you recognize that this was an innocent mistake, no harm was intended or done, and the student (and students) would benefit more from this being a teachable moment rather than an automatic enforcement of the rule regardless of the circumstances.	1. You suspend Jayden in accordance to the policy. 2. You do not suspend Jayden. His age and intent are considered. You decide this is a teachable moment for him. Instead of suspending, you talk to him and explain how he broke the school rule. You explain your rationale for not suspending Jayden to your staff. You also take this opportunity to teach the students in your school about rules, rule-breaking, intent, harm (or lack thereof), and appropriate consequences.
Example 2 Chloe, a junior in high school, insists on wearing a hoodie during class. There is an established dress code for students that indicates students should remove hats during class. However, the exception to the rule is that students of Muslim faith are allowed to wear hijabs (headwear) as part of their expression of religious freedom. Chloe is not Muslim.	Your conscience tells you that there are different approaches you might take when attending to this situation. On one hand, you need to enforce the school rule and can't make exceptions for students no matter how strongly they dislike the rule. On the other hand, you sympathize with Chloe's insecurities and rather than punishing her, you want to give her the opportunity to problem-solve without breaking the rule.	1. You inform Chloe of the policy and have her remove the hoodie. 2. You find out that Chloe wants to wear the hoodie so badly because she is embarrassed about her hair and is able to concentrate in class if she isn't worried about her appearance. You decide to meet with Chloe privately to discuss options for her so that she is not breaking the rule but is also able to concentrate in class.

Dilemma	Ethical Line	Options
Example 3 Magdalena is a second grader who is learning about life cycles in science. In addition to readings, Magdalena's teacher also provides instruction to the class about life cycles using Hopper, a rare red-legged frog who is the class pet. Each week a different student is assigned the responsibility of feeding Hopper live crickets. When it is Magdalena's turn, she secretly releases Hopper into the field next to the school playground. Magdalena is a Buddhist and killing animals violates her faith. The teacher learns that Hopper is gone and is furious because Hopper was the class pet and he is too expensive to replace. The teacher demands that you suspend Magdalena for defiance. Magdalena had not shared her religious views with the teacher.	Your conscience tells you that Magdalena shouldn't be suspended because of her age and because of her religious beliefs. On one hand, you wish that Magdalena or her parents had disclosed the family's beliefs, On the other hand, you wish that Magdalena's teacher had been more proactive in learning about each of her students. You wish that the teacher had communicated to parents that students are expected to feed live crickets to a frog, as this could be detrimental to some students regardless of faith.	1. You suspend Magdalena for defiance; this appeases the teacher and sends a message to other students that they are expected to follow all rules. 2. You convene a meeting with Magdalena and her parents to discuss the situation and how Magdalena might make amends to the teacher and her classmates. You work with the teacher to ensure this doesn't happen again by (a) informing parents of students' responsibility of feeding the frog and providing an alternate assignment for those who are unwilling and (b) having a conversation with the teacher about getting to know each of her students and their beliefs, as related to the class, curriculum, and school programs. You remind the teacher that it is her responsibility to create and maintain a safe classroom environment and a 7-year-old likely does not have the mental tools or confidence to initiate this conversation with the teacher.

WHEN MORAL COMPASSES FALTER

While some people make honest mistakes, others are guilty of premeditated dishonesty. Premeditated dishonesty includes situations that may begin as little white lies that grow into deceitful or fraudulent conduct. So, what happens if your moral compass begins to falter? When your Ethical Line becomes so faint or so blurry that you can no longer see it? "Experiments and experience show that people resist leaping from innocence to evil, but they can be lured into it one innocuous step at a time" (Chussil, 2016, p. 3).

Over time, stretching the truth or cutting corners may become habits. Life is full of slippery slopes, but by staying true to our values and commitments, we are more likely to avoid temptations that appear in our path. You might consider creating a list of things you will never do, such as looking the other way or not speaking up when you should. Writing these actions down won't safeguard you from doing something you might regret later, but it might help you to identify the beginnings of a slippery slope. The following examples, taken from the headlines, illuminate circumstances when educators ignored the slippery slope and violated ethical principles.

Cheating

One of the most well-known cheating scandals in education occurred in Atlanta in 2011. Teachers, principals, and even the superintendent were charged and found guilty of racketeering, conspiracy, and making false statements. The superintendent was the 2009 National Superintendent of the Year! She, along with hundreds of educators, were party to changing answers on state tests at erasure parties. It was reported that these parties occurred over a 10-year span, 2000–2010 (Franz, 2013) before a state review determined that some cheating had occurred in more than half of the district's elementary and middle schools (Carter, 2013). Atlanta may be the site of the most well-known cheating case, but similar situations bubbled up in New York City, El Paso, Washington, D.C., and other cities (Darden, 2014).

In 2013, 12 people were sentenced to jail time for their involvement in a cheating ring that involved 36 people in Memphis, Tennessee. The ringleader, a former teacher and assistant principal, orchestrated an elaborate scheme to help people cheat on their teacher-certification tests. Prosecutors reported that the ringleader had doctored driver's licenses and recruited teachers to impersonate others during state-required exams in three states. The ringleader accepted payment from people who wanted teaching credentials and enticed licensed teachers to take the exams using someone else's identification card. As a result, unqualified teachers were teaching students in Arkansas, Mississippi, and Tennessee (Branston, 2013).

Attendance fraud occurred in Columbus, Ohio, when school district officials from Columbus and nine other neighboring districts allegedly falsified attendance records to avoid low test scores. In this case, school leaders were accused of deflating the number of students who attended school on certain test-taking days. To avoid certain students from bringing down overall test scores, district officials disenrolled these students and then reenrolled them after the test was over (Bush, 2017).

Theft

In Detroit, a teacher was charged with gambling away thousands of dollars of student money at a local casino. The teacher was responsible for coordinating school events such as camp and homecoming. When money went missing, an audit revealed that the teacher's salary was not nearly as much as she had deposited into the penny slots. Casino receipts were found next to empty envelopes of homecoming money in the teacher's classroom. This is not an isolated incident; the district maintains a fraud hotline for employees, community members, and vendors to make reports (Hall, 2017).

Another case of theft by a school official was reported in Pennsylvania in 2018. A student council advisor confessed to stealing a student's purse and using the teenager's Victoria's Secret gift card. The purse was stolen from the student during her math class. As the story of the theft unfolded, the public also learned that the teacher was the daughter of the superintendent. In another breach of ethics, the school board had waived its anti-nepotism policy when the daughter was hired (Kellar, 2018).

Hurtful Comments

Poor behavior doesn't have to make the news in order to be unethical and harmful. There are times when our words offend others, even when there is no intention to harm. A conversation where a teacher and a clerical staff member spoke to each other in Spanish illustrates this point. The two employees were engaged in their conversation and didn't notice that the monolingual principal had entered the area. They stopped mid-sentence when the principal barked, *"Stop speaking Spanish! This isn't the swap meet."* The employees were stunned but apologized to the principal because they understood the principal to be their superior. They didn't want to risk any kind of retaliation in the future, so they stopped using their native tongue and felt devalued by their principal.

Sadly, these hurtful comments continue to be the norm in many places. This interaction between the principal and two staff members demonstrates a traditional mindset of school leadership, one where the principal has the final say. As our society and school communities become more multicultural, a shift toward cultural appreciation and responsiveness is warranted.

How Strong Is Your Moral Compass?

Unquestionably, some people have a stronger moral compass than others. Some might feel more guilt than others. One person may act dishonestly and yet feel no remorse. The next person may dwell in shame after sharing gossip. We are all wired differently.

Pay attention to the voice in your head but be selective. Don't believe everything it tells you. Our consciences vary, just as our personalities do. Some people have loud inner voices that yell at them, while others may not hear more than a whisper. Your conscience may berate you, congratulate you, or provide you with a host of reasons why or why not you might make a certain decision. At times the voice may seem to be on a running loop that you hear over and over.

Sometimes your inner voice is overpowered by outside chatter, including temptations that vie for your attention and prey upon your mental resources. Your mind is not always your best friend; you cannot trust it 100% of the time. At times our minds play tricks with us, justifying why it's OK to eat the dessert or rationalizing why it's OK to deviate from the better choice. For decisions of significance that will affect several other people, you should seek the opinions of other trusted individuals. Find a trustworthy colleague to act as your sounding board so you can talk out your options, rationales, and the various consequences of each. Be choosy; some people are terrible advisors. Choose someone who has a strong moral compass and the wisdom to view situations from different vantage points. Don't depend on whoever is available or someone who won't really "hear" you and will just placate you with quick responses to move the conversation to the next topic.

In addition to seeking counsel from a trusted colleague, it is important to develop a routine to practice self-reflection on a regular basis. When we reflect in conscious and purposeful ways, we gain additional insight into our experiences and reactions. We are able to consider how our core values furthered a cause or helped a teammate to learn and grow. Through frequent and conscious articulation, our core values become more and more natural to reference during conversations.

In the next section, we will examine the link between reflecting on core values and building mental stamina so that a meditative state is achieved. Critical components of effective and successful school leadership is the ability to lead using your head and your heart.

STRATEGY #2: BE CURIOUSLY INTROSPECTIVE

Staying true to your values and maintaining your Ethical Line is a crucial component to effective leadership. In addition to successfully managing the day-to-day operations of a school, you are also required to serve as the instructional leader. This may feel overwhelming, but these are all critical responsibilities. Your ability to practice reflective leadership and consciously manage your mental state is essential to avoid burnout. Being a principal isn't easy, so it's important to regularly take stock of how you're feeling, both physically and mentally. Establishing systems for support nourish the soul and improve your outlook during moments of uncertainty.

FIND KINDRED SPIRITS

A good leader has a support system. Nobody succeeds alone, and good leaders know that being responsive to teachers, staff, and students takes a lot of mental energy. Being present while someone confides in you is important, as people notice if you're only partially engaged or insincere or otherwise too busy for them. A true leader takes time to listen generously to others when they share personal stories. This is critical to their well-being, demonstrates their trust in your leadership, and ultimately contributes to team functioning and a positive school climate. Whether a teacher is venting or wants to unpack a delicate situation, you need to be there fully and that requires a conscious effort to maintain focus on that person's issue. Good leaders recognize that their colleagues, staff, students, and community members need them to listen intently and respond with constructive suggestions when needed. In order to be there for others, we need to make sure that we have a strong support system of our own, nourishing us so that we can be there for others. A support system may involve family members, mentors, colleagues, and others who are trustworthy and understand how to be a source of strength for you.

Since managing the helm of a school is tough work, it's important to find uplifting kindred spirits. Creating networks of kindred spirits inside and outside of your school will provide you with the crucial inspiration and support you need. Kindred spirits will ask thoughtful questions to push your thinking while also serving as your sounding board as you grapple with difficult issues. Kindred spirits don't solve your problems, but instead they provide support that helps you to process difficult decisions and prepare for hard conversations. With just a few sentiments, our kindred spirits are often able to spark new thinking for us, allowing us to discover the answers that already exist in our minds but that we haven't yet accessed. These interactions are both nourishing and productive.

PRACTICE SELF-CARE

Sometimes we tell ourselves that "it's just a cold" and to work through it, but we don't take time off of work to rest and recover properly.

Principals aren't provided a substitute, after all. Our work doesn't stop because we're sick or haven't had time to eat during the school day. Although we advise our staff members to take care of themselves, we often don't follow our own advice. While it may be difficult to take a day off, it's often necessary such that we don't allow physical symptoms to lead to cluttered thinking and poor decisions for students, not to mention worsen our own health prognosis by delaying recovery.

Willy Wonka reminds us that "a little nonsense now and then is relished by the wisest men." This advice calls to mind the notion that good leaders don't enslave others, and they don't make slaves of themselves, either. They understand that relaxation is not just a luxury but a necessity for renewal and balance. Whether it is a run, a hike in nature, or an hour at the spa, these are tools that provide emotional, physical, and spiritual self-care so that we can take better care of others.

Feeling balanced is an elusive achievement because we may feel on our game today but completely off tomorrow. Finding balance is a never-ending pursuit, but in those moments when we're there—in the zone and feeling calm—a sense of clarity is gained. Being in the zone is an energetic haven where we can slow down, take a breath, and appreciate the small but important things. During these moments, we have an opportunity to observe using all of our senses so that we can become present. Being present helps us to remain calm when life feels like it's going too fast.

Feeling present and balanced also allows us to be more effective at work. Studies show that when people reflect upon their core values, they feel less anxious during stressful experiences. In fact, this type of self-affirmation is effective for lowering stress and cortisol levels when the stakes are high and the pressure is on (Cuddy, 2015).

EXPRESS GRATITUDE

Gino and Grant (2013) assert that while everybody likes to feel appreciated, we don't say "thank you" very often, especially in our workplaces. Fifty percent of people surveyed are likely to acknowledge others who are immediately related, but only 15% of us thank our colleagues. It is startling that 35% of people reported that their managers never say "thank you." We may feel gratitude, yet we don't express it very often. It seems that a gratitude gap exists in our society.

In another study, participants were divided into three different groups and asked to keep track of their blessings, burdens, or ordinary life events. Results indicated that people who recorded things for which they were grateful also engaged in other positive, healthy behaviors such as getting more exercise. Those who counted their blessings also reported sleeping better and fewer physical illnesses than the other two groups (Emmons & McCullough, 2003).

Practicing gratitude provides physical and psychological effects, as well as deepens connections to others. Researchers assert that you don't have to write a list of things you're grateful for each day ("I'm grateful that I didn't burn dinner" or "I'm grateful that I got a good parking spot this morning"); instead, there is a greater impact when you reflect on blessings that have a bigger scope, such as "I'm grateful that my in-laws provide loving child care for us" or "I'm grateful that I have the right to vote."

Journaling is another method to organize and clarify your thoughts such that you are able to examine them in deliberate ways. This might be a daily or weekly ritual of writing freely about the day's events, or you might choose to muse over a quote, prompt, or your core values. The goal is to establish a recovery routine that fosters your ability to be healthy and resilient.

BUILD RESILIENCE

Exhaustion and burnout are the opposite of resilience. Burnout at work leaves you feeling diminished. It hurts. Tasks that were manageable now feel insurmountable. Burned out people are exhausted, overwhelmed, and often cynical (Valcour, 2016). While accomplishments are important, no one is going to award you a "busiest person ever" trophy on your deathbed.

The "key to resilience is trying really hard, then stopping, recovering, and then trying again" (Achor & Gielan, 2016). This conclusion is based on the biological concept of homeostasis. Our brain continually seeks to restore and sustain well-being. When the body is out of balance from overworking, a vast amount of mental and physical resources is used trying to regain equilibrium before we can move on.

So how do you recover and build resilience? Some might assume that if you take a break from completing tasks like answering e-mails or returning calls, you will naturally recover and be able to pick back up again later. We assume that taking a time-out will give us energy to conquer those tasks, but that's not wholly true. There is a difference between rest and recovery. Taking a time-out does not equal recovering. To build resilience at work, you need both internal and external recovery periods. Internal recovery periods take place during the workday in the form of scheduled or unscheduled short breaks when you're feeling mentally tired. During these moments, you are able to pause by shifting attention to other things. External recovery refers to actions that occur outside of work, such as having downtime or taking a vacation. Just like our bodies need rest after exertion, our brains also need to get adequate rest (Achor & Gielan, 2016).

TAKE A COGNITIVE TIME-OUT

Taking a half hour for a lunch break might feel impossible, but your body needs daily internal recovery periods. A few minutes away from your screen or the activities of the day shifts attention away from work-related issues and increases well-being. Going for a walk or spending a few minutes meditating can have powerful effects on our stress levels, fatigue, and ability to focus (Sianoja, Synek, de Bloom, Korpela, & Kinnunen, 2018).

Joe Burton is the CEO of Whil, a company that provides training for stress resilience and mental well-being. In his interview with Kira Newman (2018), he asserts that average workdays are not mindful. They are full of ongoing distractions, multitasking, and a wide range of changing emotions based upon the texts, e-mails, and calls we receive. He asserts that people often take their inability to focus and "share that as a gift with everyone else, creating this domino effect of constant distraction and interruption and checking devices 50–100 times per day" (Newman, 2018). These interruptions at work, while entertaining at times, may decrease our ability to concentrate on important tasks and hinder our ability to be fully present when a tricky issue arises.

PAUSE TO REGROUP

One tricky situation at a time is difficult enough to handle, and some-times there are occasions when multiple dilemmas present themselves at once. During these stressful situations, you may be tempted to solve one problem quickly in order to move on to the next one. Resist the urge to make snap decisions unless it's a matter of safety. While it may not feel like it in the moment, the most frequent problems that occur on campuses are not life and death situations. Typically, people want and expect a swift response from you about other important matters, and unless dire, can wait for a few hours. Don't allow pressure to compel you to make a hasty decision that you may later regret. Instead, buy yourself some time to regroup and process before making a determination.

Buying time appropriately and effectively is a skill. A less effective method of buying time is stating that you'll "get back" to them without providing a clear timeline of actions you will take and when follow-up will occur. Explicitly model your attention to each situation by listening attentively, taking notes, asking good questions, and assuring the con-cerned party that the matter is important to you, so you want to consider information from all angles. Provide three or four specific actions you will take to investigate and ask for the best number to reach them within 24 hours. When people believe that you are sincere, they will usually comply and allow you a reasonable amount of time to investigate.

CALM MENTAL CHATTER

The ability to press the pause button allows you to take a step back and calmly investigate or devise a useful plan that leads to a "win-win" situ-ation for everybody. It's more difficult to focus when you feel rushed or feel highly emotional because of an event. Having a plan to calm your mental chatter is a crucial step to making thoughtful decisions that you won't regret later.

In the following case, we learn the story of a principal (we'll call her Ms. Hale) who did not calm her mind before taking a rash action that deeply affected staff morale.

THE CASE OF THE FAILED REMODEL

Principal Hale
Elementary School
South Texas

Principal Hale was on her very last nerve because the modernization efforts to her school building were still incomplete. Although the remodel was scheduled to conclude over the summer, a number of setbacks occurred, and the construction crews were unable to finish on time. Air conditioning was one of those projects.

Instead of offering much-needed morale, Principal Hale found herself stuck, ruminating on everything that was going wrong: *"How can the front office possibly be ready for the stream of parents with questions? There is still heavy equipment in the front doorway and on the playground. How will teachers be ready, let alone provide a great first-day experience for 600 students, when they are still unpacking boxes? Will the cafeteria staff be able to feed students at lunch?"* These thoughts cycled endlessly through Principal Hale's mind and she couldn't turn them off. Her perceived lack of control manifested itself in the way she treated teachers. Principal Hale was frustrated and angry.

Since the school was almost completely gutted during the remodel, teachers were required to pack up their classrooms in June. Now that the first day of school for students was approaching, hundreds of boxes of books and classroom supplies were delivered and left outside teachers' doors early Friday morning. There was a massive effort by teachers to drag all of their boxes inside their classrooms and organize their things as quickly as possible—they only had one day to prepare, though many would probably have to come in over the weekend.

Almost all of the teachers worked through lunch, putting up bulletin boards and arranging desks in anticipation of students' arrival on Monday morning. Although the new windows were situated up high to allow natural light in the classrooms, the teachers were unable to open them. The air conditioning system was not yet functional, so some teachers had brought oscillating fans but the humidity was so high that the fans didn't do much good. The teachers, soaked in sweat, continued to prepare for Monday.

At 3:30 p.m., Principal Hale made an announcement over the PA system. She asked that all teachers meet her in the school's library at 4:00 p.m. She didn't give a reason, so several teachers concluded that Ms. Hale was going to thank them for working so hard to prepare their classroom environments in the heat. Maybe there would be some ice-cold soda or other sugary treats?

Boy, were they wrong! There was no soda, no "thank-yous," and no treats. Principal Hale had gathered the teachers to admonish them for complaining about the heat and humidity. It was true that three teachers had joked earlier that they looked more like contestants in a wet T-shirt contest than school teachers, but some sarcasm should have been expected. However, instead of shrugging off those comments or having private conversations with those three individuals, Principal Hale berated the whole teaching staff. Her admonishment made a bad situation a lot worse. Principal Hale's reputation never recovered from that day; teachers transferred to other schools as quickly as they could.

Outcome:

Principal Hale didn't pause to regroup when she felt emotional. Instead, she took out her frustration on staff members who didn't deserve to be publicly admonished. Everyone saw the way Principal Hale handled the situation and lost confidence in her ability to be a servant leader who takes care of her staff. The teachers felt unappreciated and unacknowledged for working in miserable conditions.

TOOL 1.1

Stop, Drop, and Roll

There is a remedy to the anger, angst, or confusion you might feel during a tough situation or when you feel overwhelmed by the myriad tasks to complete or people to see. Even if you prioritize balanced nutrition, exercise, and good sleeping habits to avoid making poor decisions, there may be instances when you are required to react. You don't have the luxury of journaling or phoning a friend to talk you off of the ledge.

During these times, I suggest that you follow this simple mantra that we all remember from grammar school: stop, drop, and roll. Although it was a tool we memorized to save ourselves from fire, it is also useful in other contexts to help us maintain control. This tool can be used when dealing with angry parents or unkind coworkers. The idea is to take control of your breathing, let go of your ego, and move on.

Step 1: **Stop** the mental chatter that is preventing you from being present and aware of everything that is going on around you. When your thinking feels fractured, it is unlikely that you are fully able to comprehend all of the elements of the situation at hand. When you are able to be present, your ability to consider different options increases.

Step 2: **Drop** your ego. Let it go so that you can get out of your head and take stock of the situation at hand. When you free yourself from your ego, your thinking becomes clearer. It's not about you. Your mission is to keep students' well-being at the center of all decisions. When you take your ego out of the equation, you are more likely to consider situations logically and not make hasty decisions. Choose skillful action over reaction.

Step 3: **Roll** with it. Roll with it because stress is a choice. It may not feel like it, but you always have the ability to choose your attitude. Your attitude impacts others around you and in turn shapes your school's climate and culture. As Wayne Dyer, self-development author and speaker, reminds us, "when you have a choice to be right, or to be kind, choose to be kind."

Let's consider how using the Stop, Drop, and Roll tool may have been useful to Principal Hale (and her teachers) that hot Friday afternoon:

Stop: Principal Hale might have considered setting aside her angry feelings about the teachers' comments until she was emotionally ready to have private conversations with teachers.

Drop: What is the heart of the matter? Principal Hale might have asked herself, *"What am I really upset about? Is it the teachers? Is it the weather? Is it that the construction workers are still here and school begins on Monday morning?"* Had Principal Hale paused to consider the root cause of her anxiety, she might have realized it stemmed from the condition of the school building that Friday afternoon. She might have become aware that the teachers' comments, although mildly inappropriate, were meant to make light of a miserable situation.

Roll: How might the conversations with the three teachers have gone if Principal Hale had waited until Monday to address her concerns? How might have staff morale been elevated if Principal Hale had provided some cold drinks and chocolate chip cookies on Friday afternoon? In this situation, there was nothing that Principal Hale could do to make the workers work faster. However, because of her position, Principal Hale did have a measure of influence over her teachers. She saw how hard everyone was working; she could have, and should have, said thank you. A bit of acknowledgment goes a long way.

By allowing her emotions to get the better of her, Principal Hale made a poor choice. Ultimately, that poor choice was a signal to the staff that Principal Hale was not the type of leader they wanted to work with each day. She had admonished them, and they had difficulty seeing past her actions on that day. Principal Hale failed to recognize the value of the idiom, "You'll get more with sugar than with salt." The teachers began to look for job opportunities in other schools. Ultimately, many of them transferred to other schools.

Principal Hale's situation demonstrates how she failed to acknowledge the hard work of her teachers; they felt berated. Let's take a look at another situation where a different principal (whom we'll call Ms. Soto) also faced a difficult situation but took a care-based approach.

THE CASE OF WEEKEND VANDALISM

Principal Soto
Elementary School
Northern California

It was a Sunday afternoon and Principal Soto was enjoying the warm spring afternoon by reading a book on her balcony. The phone rang and she noticed it was someone from the district office. She answered the phone, wondering what had happened. Principal Soto was informed that the school had been broken into the previous night and besides theft of school computers, five classrooms had been sprayed with paint, chairs and desks had been tossed around, and contents from the classrooms had been thrown around the room.

Principal Soto inferred from the caller that the classrooms would be unusable by teachers and students the following morning. She considered her options: (1) She could move the teachers and children from those rooms to the auditorium; (2) she could split up classrooms and disperse students to other classrooms, placing a larger burden on those teachers who would be unprepared for additional children; or (3) she could request substitute teachers so the classroom teachers could take stock of missing items and help custodians to reassemble their classrooms. The cost for securing five substitute teachers would cost the school $700, in addition to replacing items that were damaged during the break-in. Ms. Soto, like most administrators, didn't anticipate these extra costs when she designed her school budget earlier that school year, and they didn't have extra money.

So what did Principal Soto do? She chose to secure substitutes that Sunday afternoon so that the teachers could face their damaged classrooms and begin the cleanup process without having to simultaneously manage their students. The following morning the substitutes took all of the students to the auditorium and the teachers, custodians, and Principal Soto began cleaning the classrooms. Although the school had been vandalized, which hurt everyone's feelings, the teachers were able to clean up and prepare for Tuesday morning with their students.

Principal Soto reviewed the school budget and identified how the $700 used for substitutes might be recovered without affecting students or staff. Since there wasn't any extra money, Principal Soto contacted the local Walmart and informed the store manager about the vandalism. The store manager agreed to donate paint, paper, and other classroom supplies, helping to make up for the money spent on substitutes. That week, and for weeks to come, Principal Soto's decision to arrange substitutes improved staff morale and demonstrated her compassion to the school community.

> Outcome: *Principal Soto had to choose between staying within the budget and doing what was best for teacher and student morale. She chose to exceed the budget but found a way to make up the funds elsewhere.*
>
> Takeaway: *Principal Soto's choice to arrange for substitute teachers brought peace of mind to her teachers and students. They were able to heal from the feeling that their school and their things had been violated. Principal Soto's gesture of providing subs signaled her understanding of the unease that teachers and students felt. It was an offering of one way to make a hurtful situation better.*

Being a school principal can be challenging at times, so it's important to acknowledge the many ways you positively impact the school community. Undoubtedly, you will make mistakes; we all do. The ability to learn from your mistakes will help you to become the thoughtful and skilled leader that our students need and deserve. Don't be too hard on yourself. Your ability to stop, drop, and roll like Principal Soto will reduce the number of minutes, or hours, that you might otherwise spend fretting about a problematic situation.

DARE TO IMAGINE

"The job of the school principal has never been an easy one, with increased accountability making it even more challenging and the stakes higher than ever before" (Alvoid & Black, 2014, p. 28), and 75% of principals believe the job has become too complex (MetLife, 2013). Surviving, and thriving, in today's school settings require that principals know themselves well. Modeling your core values and continually reflecting are two strategies that effective and successful leaders utilize to be purposeful, stay mentally sharp, and advance the school's mission.

Ultimately, adhering to our values and practicing reflective leadership enables principals to become survivalists—the leaders our diverse students and communities need us to be. We have skin in the game. Called by a larger purpose, we can form alliances that unite people around a shared purpose. We can nourish ourselves and support each other along this journey. That you've picked up this book is a signal that you are the right person to lead the charge at your school. Dare to imagine how much better your work and outcomes for your students can be.

Before moving on to Chapter 2, clarify your purpose and mission by considering these questions:

ACTIVITY 1.2

Who Are You as a Leader?

I became an educational leader because . . .
The leadership values that I live by are . . .
My leadership vision is . . .
When making tough decisions, I evaluate my options by . . .
You will be able to see this at my school when . . .

ACTIVITY 1.3

How Do You Make Decisions?

My responsibility to students' physical, emotional, and social well-being is evidenced by . . .
I seek counsel from . . .
I seek counsel when . . .
My commitment to actualizing all students' learning is seen when . . .
My responsibility to my district is . . .
I demonstrate my values to my school community when . . .
You will be able to see my ethics in action when . . .

EXAMINE YOUR COMMUNITY'S VALUES

As we learned in Chapter 1, a chief responsibility of any school principal is to lead others by modeling your core values. Being aware of your Ethical Line will provide you with the perspective you will need to effectively manage the challenging complexities of today's schools. Chapter 2 connects your understanding of your Ethical Line to how your school community perceives your leadership and how you, in turn, understand and honor the values of your community. Part of examining the values of your community is making a concerted effort to listen more than you talk (Strategy #3), build school climates where people feel valued and respected (Strategy #4), reaching out to create partnerships among community members (Strategy #5), and ultimately unify staff and community members by co-developing a collective vision (Strategy #6). These four strategies work together, furthering your mission to be an ethical leader who makes the effort to know your community and serve their needs.

STRATEGY #3: LISTEN GENEROUSLY

CHARACTERISTICS OF OUTSTANDING LISTENERS

Education leaders face challenging ethical decisions on a regular basis, making it important that we carefully tune into what is being voiced by staff and community members, as well as ask thoughtful questions that uncover hidden agendas. While we go through our lives engaging in conversation with friends, family members, and coworkers, when asked, most adults believe they possess above-average listening skills because they know not to talk when others are speaking, they repeat back what the speaker has said, and they use facial expressions and verbal sounds such as "mmm-hmm" to show they're listening (Zenger & Folkman, 2016). However, much of the time we don't listen nearly as well as we could or maybe even should. Frequently we're distracted by lights and sounds from our phones, tablets, and televisions, and while we might get the gist of a conversation, we're not really giving the other person our full attention.

While long identified as an important communication skill in all facets of life, including the workplace, active listening is considered an underutilized management skill (Daimler, 2016). Active listening differs from passive listening or simple hearing by establishing a "deeper connection between speaker and listener, as the listener gives the speaker full attention via inquiry, reflection, respect, and empathy" (Spataro & Bloch, 2018, p. 168). While therapists are often mocked for being active listeners, scientific evidence supports that this technique increases the quality of interactions with others (Grohol, 2018). Being a good listener requires, at minimum, active listening and demonstrating genuine empathy. Listening generously is essential to ethical leadership because in order to make sound decisions, we need to know the facts. We must listen for what is being said and what is being omitted so that we ask the right follow-up questions.

TOOL 2.1

Active Listening

A two-way exchange of information is the goal of active listening. The listener should develop a clear understanding of the speaker's message while clearly communicating his interest in the speaker's message through specific behaviors including paraphrasing, attentive body language, and by maintaining eye contact. Weger, Bell, Minei, and Robinson (2014) define active listening as having three essential components:

1. The listener's nonverbal engagement that indicates full attention

2. The listener reflects the speaker's message back to the speaker

3. The listener encourages elaboration and further details through questioning

Zenger and Folkman (2016) reported findings following a study of managers seeking to become better coaches. In this analysis, the researchers identified four main themes that differentiate average listeners from outstanding listeners.

Outstanding Listeners

1. Ask questions that foster discovery and insight

2. Have the ability to build a person's self-esteem

3. Are adept at providing feedback that results in a shared dialogue

4. Have an ability to make good suggestions that illuminate other paths the speaker might consider

Outstanding listeners periodically ask questions that foster discovery and insight. Posed thoughtfully, these questions may challenge old assumptions or foster new understandings. Silently nodding while some-one talks doesn't assure that someone is truly listening, but good questions lets the speaker know that his message was comprehended well enough to want additional information. The best conversations are reciprocal exchanges instead of a one-way "speaker versus hearer" interaction.

The second characteristic of outstanding listeners is their ability to build a person's self-esteem. In these exchanges, the speaker had a positive experience that is unlikely if the listener is passive or critical. These types of conversations promote a safe space where issues and differences in opinion are openly discussed. Excellent listeners make the other person feel supported while conveying confidence in them.

In addition to providing a positive experience for the speaker, outstanding listeners are also adept at providing feedback to the speaker that results in a shared dialogue. Dialogue is characterized here by both speaker and listener building on each other's ideas. In these conversations, thoughts and questions go both directions and neither party feels vexed or hurt by the other's comments. In comparison, poor listeners are seen as competitors who listened with the intent of identifying errors or used their silence to prepare their next response. While this might be a good skill for a debate, it doesn't make you a good listener. The speaker wants to feel like you're trying to help, not like you're trying to win an argument.

The final behavior exhibited by outstanding listeners is their ability to make good suggestions that illuminate other paths the speaker might consider. By contrast, sometimes we hear complaints such as, "So-and-so didn't want to listen to me. He just wanted to solve the problem." Accordingly, the way in which suggestions are made is critically important to the speaker's assessment of the conversation.

"Listening creates spaciousness, which we need to do good work" (Daimler, 2016) and while it may seem like a straightforward leadership skill, the number of books devoted to listening reflects the widespread need for it (Spataro & Bloch, 2018). As an ethical leader, you'll want to continually be aware of and hone your outstanding listening skills to make sure you are lifting up everyone in your school community and not missing out on essential information or nuances affecting the climate and culture of your school. The table in Figure 2.1 lists some

Figure 2.1   Barriers to Effective Conversations

	Barrier	Example
1	Asking questions that make the speaker defensive	"Why did you that?" "What were you thinking?"
2	Minimizing the speaker's opinion or feelings	Offering quick reassurance, such as "It's nothing. Don't worry about it."
3	Giving advice	"I think you should . . ."
4	Prying, gossiping, or meddling	"Did you hear about . . ."
5	Belittling	"You'll be fine."
6	Preaching	"You need to . . ."

barriers to effective conversations that you'll want to avoid or take steps to prevent.

Being mindful of these impediments to effective conversations might help you to avoid those errors and create spaces for meaningful conversations. Further, active listeners project more positive impressions and are perceived to be friendlier, more trustworthy, and understanding than less effective listeners (Weger et al., 2014). To move our schools forward, we must be willing to listen, meet people where they are, and compromise. Being observant of these impediments to effective conversations, and actively fighting them, enhances your ability to be more compassionate and empathetic to others.

PRACTICE EMPATHY

According to the Greater Goods Science Center at the University of California, Berkeley, empathy is the ability to detect other people's emotions, combined with the ability to visualize what someone else might be thinking or feeling. These researchers contend that empathic people are typically more generous and are concerned with others' well-being. Empathic people tend to have greater personal well-being and be involved in happier relationships than others. Empathy is seen as a way to facilitate effective communication and improve leadership ability (Haiyan & Walker, 2014).

Scientists from UC Berkeley contend that we have different amounts of empathy in our personalities. If you're wondering how empathetic you are, there is a free quiz you can take (see Activity 2.1). If your score does not indicate that you are an empathic person, the site offers suggestions, including ways to practice active listening, how to find commonalities with others, and paying attention to facial expressions. "One of the first ways to build empathy is to hone your powers of observation and cultivate the ability to see what others overlook" (Gallagher & Thordarson, 2018, p. 23). With so much input around us, we are prone to screening out details; while we can't assimilate everything, it's important to be mindful of the information we take in so that it can be accessed at a later time.

ACTIVITY 2.1

1. Take the empathy quiz from *Greater Good Magazine*: https:// greatergood.berkeley.edu/quizzes/take_quiz/empathy.

2. Follow up with at least one of the after-quiz suggestions for becoming even more empathetic.

STRATEGY #4: CREATE AN INCLUSIVE SCHOOL CLIMATE

PROMOTE EMOTIONAL WELL-BEING

Part of being an ethical leader is ensuring the emotional health and wellness of your staff. Emotions are contagious. Daniel Goleman asserts that the leader is a group's emotional guide and has the power to sway people's emotions (2004). When a leader feels enthusiastic, and pushes others' emotions toward enthusiasm, performance may soar. Have you noticed that your mood is often affected by that of your supervisor?

How have your previous managers created a climate of belonging in the workplace? How do you strategically create a climate of belonging in your school?

Quaglia and Corso (2016) assert that "schools are like finger-prints—no two are alike. And so it is with leadership in schools; you must tailor your skills and adapt your knowledge to best meet the needs of your school" (p. 24). How do you determine the needs and wants of your staff? While having an open-door policy is a strong practice, make it a priority to visit teachers and staff members on their turf. Offer to meet in their classrooms or in other common areas and be prepared to ask thoughtful, open-ended questions. When approached

> While having an open-door policy is a strong practice, make it a priority to visit teachers and staff members on their turf.

authentically, these conversations will help you to understand your staff's needs at deeper levels. You will also gain insight into how each person ticks and learn what is important to him or her. These exchanges are ideal times to acknowledge the person's work, inquire about challenges, and celebrate successes. As the old saying goes, *"People don't care about what you know, they care about how you make them feel."*

Be Authentic

Have you ever pretended to be knowledgeable about a topic, hoping that the other person wouldn't find out you were confused? Have you kept personal stories to yourself for fear of being judged? We all have experienced occasions such as these. We cross our fingers and hope that we won't be found out because we wish to appear more than we really are. While we may escape judgment temporarily, people will soon recognize a fake. To make a difference in the lives of students, we must be willing to bring our whole selves to our school communities. This means being humble, authentic, and recognizing that we're all vulnerable human beings. We are imperfect but doing the best we can.

Being authentic is demonstrated by the courage to ask for help, speak up, and connect with others in a genuine way, allowing our true selves to be seen (Robbins, 2018). Your ability to connect with people is enhanced when you are open and honest. When we are honest about our imperfections, we can be more fully present to ask sincere questions. Keep in mind that if you believe in being a lifelong learner and use an inquiry approach to develop your own capacity, no one will accuse you of being incompetent. Instead of masking your true self, try modeling curiosity earnestly.

How will you support the authentic growth and learning of the adults on your campus? People are watching to see if you praise their efforts or if you punish them for mistakes or when they come up short. Since your attitude toward employees can be seen and felt, help them to identify and remedy any growth areas and celebrate their accomplishments. Although the browbeater may see some changes in behavior, the cheerleader will boost morale while reinforcing desired behaviors.

Since all eyes are on the leader, it is important that you radiate positive emotions toward others. Cultivate these skills in your teachers and staff, as they will transfer to students. Nurture skills such as cooperation, perseverance, and empathic listening such that everyone wants to be a part of the team. Tasks that seem dull can be envisioned differently with an infusion of enthusiasm and appreciation. Although knowledge and skills matter, your attitude toward students, colleagues, and the community are equally, if not more, important than your ability to drive a team toward an established goal. Your proficiency as an emotionally in-tune leader is critical to your school's overall success.

Establish Trust

People are watching you to determine how they feel about you and if they want to be a part of your team. How do you develop trust? How do you cultivate an inclusive climate? From an evolutionary standpoint, people prioritize warmth over competence because it is crucial to survival. We instinctively want to know whether or not we can trust someone (Cuddy, 2015). Instead of speculating about others' perspectives, ask for their input. When you regularly engage your staff in purposeful discussions that are relevant to the school's mission, you are building ownership and deepening trust.

Two-way conversations also deepen trust and provide learning opportunities for both people. Leaders should seek to understand another's point of view before providing advice that you think might be helpful. Instead, ask for permission to share a personal experience if you think it will be useful. Remember, it's not about you. By allowing the other person to steer the conversation, you will learn much more and deepen trust.

Solicit Feedback Early and Often

There are a number of ways to engage staff and community members in school business and functions. People appreciate opportunities to provide feedback about their children's school year or comment on school culture. Students as young as kindergarten can respond to surveys about classroom and school climate, if they feel cared for by their teacher, and what they think of school lunches. Surveys, such as Student Voice (Quaglia, Corso, Fox, & Dykes, 2017), are tools that many schools use to solicit input on a regular basis.

Ideas for Engaging the School Community

- Surveys
- Pose school-wide questions to solicit feedback
- Encourage participation in community service projects
- Provide platforms where community members can share their ideas
- Invite community members from all aspects of the school (e.g., cafeteria workers, cleaning staff, clerical staff, teachers, students, parents, local residents, neighborhood business owners) to participate in meetings and conversations

Although this takes effort on the part of the principal, it is time well spent because those investments will reap immediate and long-term rewards. In addition to deeper insight, consistency and trust are built during these exchanges. In the absence of a trusting environment, people may nod with half-hearted agreement but take no ownership of issues.

Inevitably, problematic situations will arise and you must attend to conflicts. Instead of avoiding these issues, determine how you will respond. Recognize when you are feeling stressed and take proactive self-care measures such as those mentioned in Chapter 1. Knowing your triggers and predetermining how you will respond in any given situation will help you to remain calm and consistent. Undoubtedly, there will be times when you're really angry or upset. Since the leader sets the tone for the school climate, it's important to understand how your emotions can transfer to others around you such that you minimize any negative signals to students, staff, and the community.

ENGENDER TEAMWORK

Leadership is a team sport. Developing systems of teaching and learning is not something that the principal should approach alone. It means getting everyone on board to reach agreed-upon goals. Often when there isn't agreement, understanding, or ownership to a decision, plan, or initiative, the result can be seen by the inaction that follows. Savvy and ethical principals understand they need to engage people in meaningful dialogue that fosters an inclusive participation regarding curricular decisions, activities and functions, and school governance.

Although the principal is charged with making key decisions, in most cases the district and community would not prefer that the decisions be made in isolation. Leadership guru John Maxwell asserts, "If it's lonely at the top, you're not doing something right" (2012), suggesting that it's critical for leaders to engage other people in discussions. In most cases, the urgent decisions that the principal might make without asking for input are related to safety and privacy.

A note about safety and privacy: It's important that the principal has communicated the school policies for these circumstances because there will be times when confidential information can't be shared with staff or the public. Once again, use of a handbook to house standard policies that serve as the backbone for all administrative decisions can be useful. The practice of following established policies provides consistency to all members of the school community, including the principal.

Procedures that are viewed as fair and equitable contribute to a healthy school climate.

"Leadership is one part leader and nine parts team" (Toler, 2015, p. 83). While principals should have personal and professional goals, and strive to excel individually, their greatest achievements are building teams. Greater participation breeds greater success.

FACILITATE COLLABORATIVE LEADERSHIP

Collaborative leadership centers around working with and empowering others to co-develop goals and activities. It is also the "purposeful actions we take as leaders to enhance the instruction of teachers, build deep relationships with all stakeholders, and deepen our learning together" (DeWitt, 2017, p. 4). It is the totality of instruc-

> Collaborative leadership centers around working with and empowering others to co-develop goals and activities.

tional and transformational leadership, as well as administrative duties, that accompany managing a school.

Leading together does not mean manipulating people to agree with the predetermined goals we have already settled on. A collaborative leader uses evidence to meet stakeholders where they are, models those practices, and motivates them to improve. Co-developing observation cycles and professional development agendas with teachers are examples of collaborative leadership. Parents are also included in conversations because they can tell us about the ways their children learn. When appropriate, collaborative leaders give voice to students and include them in decision-making processes (DeWitt, 2017).

Listening generously and taking in the information from all sources is crucial to developing an organic leadership framework for your site that demonstrates that you are one part of the decision-making body at the school. Staff are empowered to make decisions that are responsive to the community's specific needs because you have created the conditions that unify stakeholders around a central vision (Alvoid & Black,

2014). In other words, collaborative leadership is realized when the principal and staff coordinate and take action steps together.

RECOGNIZE THE SIGNS OF AN UNHEALTHY SCHOOL CLIMATE

Without conditions that spark productive discussion and engagement, people may feel silenced or have the impression that the school climate is repressive. Inconsistency or authoritarianism on the part of the principal means that people and situations may receive differentiated attention, support, and resources. When teachers and staff feel muzzled, they are afraid to speak up during the day, so they may complain to each other in the parking lot after school. It also means that people don't feel valued and may only half-heartedly participate in school functions, let alone provide engaging classroom environments for students. It's not to say that teachers will abandon their nurturing ways to students, but when staff feels mistrustful of their principal, students feel it. It starts at the top and rubs off on staff. See Figure 2.2 for signals of an unhealthy school climate and one that is healthy.

Another sign of a stifled school culture is seen when the principal uses a top-down approach, issuing commands and directives. In these schools staff watch to see who gets punished and who is rewarded by the principal. In this climate, teachers may do their own thing while staying within parameters controlled by the principal such that they aren't scolded or chewed out. Staff under these conditions are less likely to engage in the conversations necessary to develop systems of teaching and learning.

In the case of the Dual Immersion Debacle that follows, we learn how the school culture, and ultimately student achievement, was negatively impacted by the actions of the leader we'll call Principal Nash. Ms. Nash was of the opinion that she knew what was best for her school community and made decisions without considering input from teachers, even when they voiced their concerns.

Figure 2.2 Stifled and Vibrant School Climate Indicators

CM = Community members

Signs of a Stifled School Climate	Signs of a Vibrant School Climate
CM feel silenced.	CM feel invited to share their thoughts and opinions.
CM do not trust the principal.	CM trust the principal to listen generously.
CM believe that the principal will retaliate against those who express differing opinions.	CM feel welcomed to share their opinion without fear of retribution.
CM believe that the principal plays favorites with some and ignores others.	CM trust the principal to treat all stakeholders with equal care and concern for their well-being.
CM complain among each other in private and off campus.	CM feel free to come to the principal with concerns.
Staff does not feel valued.	Staff trust that the principal values them as individuals and as professionals.
Voluntary participation and morale is low.	CM feel motivated to participate wholeheartedly in school activities.
The principal issues commands and directives.	The principal leads collaboratively.
Staff resist engaging in conversations to develop systems of teaching and learning.	Staff enthusiastically initiate conversations to improve systems of teaching and learning.
Staff are more compliance oriented.	Staff feel empowered to be creative and active participants.
Staff feel detached from school initiatives.	CM feel a sense of ownership in the school.
Staff are resigned that nothing will change.	Staff feel hopeful that they can actively contribute to school improvement.

THE CASE OF THE DUAL
IMMERSION DEBACLE

Principal Nash
Elementary School
Utah

At a school we'll call Cheshire Elementary School, student enrollment had been dropping steadily for years. The reason for the decrease in enrollment was due to the location of the school on the well-established west side of the city. The homes in the area no longer had school-age children living there and due to its proximity to the mountains, there was nowhere for new homes to be built. The drop of enrolled students had a negative impact on the school's budget and therefore student services. Some teachers (Science, Art, Spanish) were reduced from full-time positions to part-time positions. The school bookkeeper and various paraprofessionals also had their hours cut. Something had to be done to increase enrollment.

Principal Nash held meeting after meeting with the community and the staff to determine ways to approach this problem. It was decided that Cheshire needed to specialize in something that would draw families to attend the school. Various ideas were discussed, including STEM, environmental education, and Spanish immersion. Although most community members and teachers wanted Cheshire to become a STEM school, Principal Nash decided to make Cheshire a Spanish immersion school. She had attended a language immersion conference and felt strongly that immersion could work for Cheshire. Many teachers and parents expressed concerns about Spanish immersion: Where would they find enough qualified bilingual teachers? How would they afford Spanish curriculum? How would parents be able to support their children with homework in Spanish? How would teachers be trained in immersion teaching techniques? How would the needs of Special Education students be addressed in Spanish? Principal Nash avoided the hard issues and stated that the school would work through everything as needs arose. There appeared to be no pre-planning ahead of this drastic curricular change at Cheshire.

This unilateral decision on Principal Nash's part was the beginning of a 10-year disaster for Cheshire Elementary. Although Principal Nash received advice to wait a year before starting Spanish immersion to allow for proper training and materials to be purchased, she pushed the immersion program to begin with only five months preparation, and nearly three of those months were summer vacation. In order to register enough children for the immersion program, Principal Nash contacted parents personally and applied pressure on them to enroll their children. A lottery was created to determine which students would be enrolled. However, Principal Nash refused to allow the lottery to be public and suspicions arose about the results when it was revealed that the first immersion class was extremely unbalanced; it was filled with students of high academic capabilities and lacked any students with special needs. Principal Nash refused to answer any questions from parents or her staff. As a matter of fact, staff members who questioned the Spanish immersion program were harassed and accused of being dissentious to the climate of Cheshire.

Spanish immersion did bring in more families to Cheshire and enrollment did rise for the first few years of the program. Principal Nash took great pride in "her" program and increased the number of Spanish-language classrooms. She then required that literacy skills be taught in Spanish, not English. According to her research, she felt that students could learn to read in Spanish and that it would increase their English skills as well. The flaw with her reasoning was that she only used research that supported her idea—ignoring the research that claimed Spanish literacy would not automatically transfer to English literacy skill development in children, although many staff members tried to share their concerns with her. Once again, dissenting opinions were squelched and those teachers felt ostracized.

After two years of students receiving all their instruction, including literacy, in Spanish, the standardized test scores began dropping. The number of students who needed intense reading intervention increased to the point where the school could not meet all the needs of students who could not read. Still, Principal Nash refused to change the full immersion model she had pushed into place. Parents began to realize that their children could not read although they were now in second grade and made appointment after appointment to talk to her. Parents were frustrated with Principal Nash's irrational dedication to an immersion program that obviously was not working—students could neither read in English or Spanish! Realizing that Principal Nash would never acknowledge her errors or change the program, families began to pull their children out of Cheshire—even in the middle of the school year. Cheshire lost 60 families in one semester.

Finally, the district administration took notice of the plight of Cheshire. Previously, the district had allowed the site the freedom to make their own decisions with little interference from the district. Parents and teachers organized themselves and presented written testimonials and documentation of Principal Nash's ineffective administration to the district leadership. Within one day of receiving this information, Principal Nash was forced to retire from her position as principal of Cheshire Elementary.

Given what we know about the importance of listening and creating a climate where information and ideas are shared freely, what steps might the principal of Cheshire have taken to ensure that the staff and school community were involved in the development of a new program? How might the principal of Cheshire have provided a different response when teachers and parents voiced their concern for the program?

When Principal Nash decided to make programmatic changes to the school, she failed to involve staff and community in the discussions and planning. She attended a workshop about dual immersion and was convinced that this program would be a great accomplishment for the school and would attract new families. While dual immersion can be beneficial to students, the community had wanted STEM education. Ultimately, Principal Nash's unilateral decision making led to a failure of leadership. Student enrollment dwindled, achievement dropped, and school culture suffered. Principal Nash was removed from the school and elected to retire from education.

STIMULATE A HEALTHY SCHOOL CLIMATE

School leaders can choose to purposefully design a culture that values the input and insight of each member of the school community, or they can settle for a lackluster school culture. Which would you prefer for your school? People want to contribute and feel valued and respected by their principal and in their school communities—this is what some might call a community of collective inquiry.

Thoughtful human interactions will lead to a positive school climate. As an ethical leader, foster dialogues that are critical spaces to surface and challenge assumptions. Encourage dialogues as opportunities to raise questions, negotiate meaning and implications, share essential information, and progress toward agreement and consensus. In the case study that follows you'll learn about a principal (we'll call her Ms. Ross and we'll call the school Clark Middle School) who conducted empathetic interviews to collect necessary information about school morale and how to improve it.

THE CASE OF THE RENEWED TEAM SPIRIT

Principal Ross
Middle School
Southern California

By conducing empathetic interviews, Principal Ross learned that student achievement and staff morale were low. Teachers discussed their frustration with a diverse, yet apathetic student body and she sensed a lack of instructional cohesion. The staff felt demoralized by previous administrators who had admonished them because of the low achievement scores. A fifth-grade teacher confided that the staff felt like they had PTSD (posttraumatic stress disorder). During interviews with students, Principal Ross learned that students felt bored in class but had an appetite to learn. Parents told her how they wanted their kids to be successful and have better lives than they did. These conversations signaled that the pieces of a healthy school climate were present but needed some polish.

Principal Ross began dialogues about teaching and learning with staff, students, and parents. She used her core values to invoke a sense of unity and began to create situations to spark learning, jump-start a healthy school climate, and breathe new life into the system. Early wins led to enthusiasm, renewed feeling of purpose, and a sense of team spirit. Staff was smiling, kids formed their own book clubs, and parents began to volunteer in classrooms like never before. Together, they looked at student work, investigated and selected curriculum, and jointly developed a plan designed to build instructional excellence and keep kids engaged at school. Sure enough, attendance rates went up and disciplinary referrals went down. The silver bullet was understanding the people—the staff, students, and parents—and deliberately appealing to their need to be an actively contributing member of a winning team.

Dialogue was critical to the health of the school climate, and ultimately student achievement. Principal Ross understood the quality of dialogue shapes how people gather and process information, how they make decisions, how they feel about each other, and how they feel about the quality of the decisions that affect the school community. Dialogue offers the opportunity to generate new ideas and improved outcomes, as seen at Clark Middle School. The content and tone of dialogue influences people's beliefs and behaviors, essentially becomes the school culture, more quickly and more permanently than any vision statement, structural change, or reward system. To this day, student achievement and school culture continue to thrive at Clark Middle School because dialogue is ongoing and frequent; norms and shared commitments are discussed and reaffirmed regularly.

FOSTER COLLECTIVE EFFICACY

Jenni Donohoo, an expert on collective efficacy, asserts that when staffs engage in productive behaviors that support student learning, positive school environments are promoted and students feel good about themselves. "The strength of collective efficacy beliefs affects how school staffs tackle difficult challenges" (Donohoo, 2017, p. 13). Collective efficacy should be at the forefront of any planned strategic effort in a school or district. Building these structures requires teamwork; the key here is that it is a collective effort, not an individual one.

> **Collective Efficacy:** A group of people can be said to have collective efficacy when they believe that their collective actions can positively improve student outcomes, and that through their collective efforts student achievement will increase (Donohoo, 2017).

Collective efficacy has been shown to produce many benefits, including greater effort and persistence, a willingness to try new approaches, and an internal accountability system that promotes high expectations. Formal Communities of Practice, as well as informal conversations in hallways, become the norm when there is a sense of collective efficacy. Relational trust among the staff is deepened, and these connections set the tone for the whole school.

In an inclusive culture, leaders ensure that lunch room chatter, committee meetings, conferences, trainings, and other social structures on campus operate in inclusive ways. These day-to-day interactions in schools serve as a catalyst to advance the school culture. Promoting positive group norms, expectations, and social structures creates spaces for reaching and executing decisions collaboratively. Done correctly, this will lead to internal accountability where every community member feels accountable to the school community as a whole.

STRATEGY #5: DISCOVER YOUR COMMUNITY'S HOPES AND DREAMS

Principals serve many stakeholder groups simultaneously: parents, community members, students, teachers, and central office staff. Each of these interest groups have their own needs and expectations that can clash and cause friction. Strategy #5 offers steps for discovering the hopes and dreams of your community members, sharing your own hopes and dreams with them, and for examining your hidden biases.

EXPLORE COMMUNITY ASSETS AND EXAMINE YOUR LEADERSHIP PRIVILEGE

To more deeply understand students' needs and the needs of the community surrounding the school, take a drive (or better yet, walk) around the neighborhood and notice the services that are available to families as well as services that aren't. Is this a neighborhood you would want to live in with your family? Do the assets of the neighborhood cause you to judge your students and their parents negatively or positively? A systematic assessment of your community, its procedures, and codes will provide you with concrete data regarding what the community values, as well as uncover the hopes and dreams the community has for their children. In doing so, you might discover opportunities where the school and surrounding community can work together to accomplish mutual goals.

When you walk around the neighborhood, you will likely get a "sense of privilege or deprivation" (Terrell & Lindsey, 2009) regarding the assets that contribute (positively or negatively) to students' achievement and well-being. How can you examine your own unspoken sentiments regarding people of color, class, culture, sexual orientation, and religion in a way that makes you more open toward facilitating reciprocal relationships that benefit all members of the community?

School and district leaders carry considerable administrative privilege. If you are not mindful and critically self-reflective, educators run the risk of acting in oppressive ways toward community opinions and needs (Khalifa, 2018). Understanding your school and community is a two-way process. Community members want to know about you: Who you are as an educator and human being. What makes you tick? Why are you entering their community and why should they care? Identify the guiding principles that undergird your motives and share them with your community.

TAKE THE PULSE OF YOUR COMMUNITY REGULARLY

Processes for ongoing examination of your community and your organization's values will help you gauge internal and external expectations and perceptions of your leadership and the direction of the school. Don't rely on speculations or expect a group or an individual to behave as they once did. Make it a regular practice to check in with your stakeholders to understand and assess how current events, both local and on a national level, are affecting your community.

> The ability to be empathetic and examine issues from the point of view of others, especially those from different backgrounds, is critical to ethical leadership.

Many of us believe that others see the world as we do, but in reality, the worldviews of others differ from our own. The ability to be empathetic and examine issues from the point of view of others, especially those from different backgrounds, is critical to ethical leadership. Being inquisitive and asking probing questions of community members is useful to illuminate blind spots and less visible information that you might not otherwise see. The likelihood of generating a solution that is responsive to all facets of the problem decreases when a singular approach is utilized. Soliciting community input is also an effective way to establish support once a decision is made.

Events that occur outside of school might be mirrored in schools by students who grapple with the emotions that accompany adolescence. Parents and students are more likely to confide in us when they believe the school climate is inclusive and supportive (DeWitt, 2017). Politics and volatile situations spread across social media might trigger a shift in an organization or community's views. By keeping an eye on current trends and being thoughtfully inquisitive, we send a signal that the issues in the community are issues to us. For example, both perceived and real police violence toward African American teenagers demonstrate how current events impact community perception of law enforcement (Stoughton, 2016). Actions that might have been considered taboo 10 or 20 years ago might appear to be more acceptable now. Instead of making assumptions of what is on the minds of your community members, it's important to ask firsthand. The responses might surprise you.

EMPATHIC INTERVIEWING

Empathetic interviews are authentic conversations that allow you to identify an individual's needs and desires. It's not an interview in a formal sense, but rather it is a conversation that is designed to elicit information. Whereas surveys are designed to quickly gather information from large groups and are useful for analyzing data, they do not allow us to understand why an individual or group of people answered a question in a certain way. "Empathic interviews are designed to gather deep information about fewer people's experiences" (Gallagher & Thordarson, 2018, p. 29). During empathy interviews, the interviewer first establishes rapport and then works to understand the person's lived experience through story. This technique means that you open dialogue by asking "why?" frequently. Resist the urge to make assumptions, because even if you think you know the answer, sometimes the explanations provided might surprise you. Empathic interviews are opportunities to move from abstract conversations to authentic interactions.

Empathic interviewing is a skill. If you approach these interactions haphazardly, you may unintentionally offend people. It's difficult to recover once you offend someone, so spend time intentionally crafting a strategy that communicates your core values within the context of what it is you want to know. Unless you conscientiously provide the guiding principles and reasons behind your inquiries, key information may not be shared with you. Empathy is a two-way street, so listen generously and be vulnerable and willing to share aspects about yourself.

Share what you think you already know about this school and community. Explain what you are trying to learn and why. You may choose to begin with quantitative data that you find online or you might start by interviewing people to soak up their narratives. Tool 2.2 provides a framework for empathic interviewing to consider when creating a strategy for learning more about your school community.

TOOL 2.2

Preparing for Empathic Interviews

Reflection questions to help you craft your strategy and guiding principles

Core Values	What do you stand for? How do you demonstrate and articulate your values? Do your words and actions telegraph a cohesive message to others?
Background	What do you already know about this school and community? How do you know? How might your own context impact the school community? What assumptions might you need to examine?

Purpose	What are you trying to learn and why? What are your guiding principles for being a leader in this school? What is your purpose?
People	Who are the people who have historical knowledge of the school? Who are the key personalities you need to talk to? Is there a power base? What factions of people exist, and what are their concerns?
Actions	What are your goals for the school and the education of its students? What steps are needed and in what order? What support will you need from the school community to reach these goals?
Measures	What sources will you seek out for honest, ongoing feedback?

After developing your strategy to address what you're trying to learn, where will you start? The great thing about empathic interviewing is that you can do it anywhere, anytime. It may seem simple, but these conversations are very powerful. Through narrative, we can determine if our reading intervention efforts are working. We can discern whether parents want to start a lacrosse team. What do parents wish you knew about their kids? You will likely come across interesting insights when you spend time with the people whose lives are impacted by the school.

In addition to getting to know the people of your community, it is also important to take the time to explore the neighborhood. Look for the physical structures that exist in the area, as well as search for the less obvious, intangible connections and partnerships that may benefit students and the school one day. Activity 2.2 offers some guiding questions to help you in this endeavor.

ACTIVITY 2.2

Neighborhood Asset Inventory

How many churches or houses of worship are in your community? What religions do they represent?	
Who are the current community partners with whom the school works? Which students do these partnerships serve?	
What potential partnerships, including community-based organizations, for-profit businesses, and faith-based organizations, are present?	

Once you gather information from your Neighborhood Asset Inventory, you will have a deeper understanding of organizations that may share common interests with those of the school. These may be future partners in your students' education and might provide you with insight into the needs and desires of community members. Information that you gather from the staff and community, coupled with codes of conduct from your organization, will assist you to lead the charge to shape a collective vision that is collaboratively developed with your school community.

STRATEGY #6: UNIFY AROUND A COLLECTIVE VISION

WHICH VALUES GUIDE YOUR ORGANIZATION?

In all facets of life, codes exist because society agrees that there is a need for a system of rules and laws. Beyond laws, people have pointed out a need for standards of ethical conduct. Songwriters such as Aretha Franklin ("Truth and Honesty") and Tom Petty ("I Won't Back Down") remind us to be truthful and stand up for what we believe in. We teach our children about the importance of telling the truth through fables of long ago and through current events such as when Dr. Christine Blasey Ford testified against then-nominated Supreme Court Justice Brett Kavanaugh. Telling the truth was costly; it damaged her reputation, safety, and her privacy, but she felt compelled to tell the truth. Declarations like these are life skills that remind kids, as well as adults, to always uphold your values and to follow the golden rule. Even crooks depend on "honor among thieves" and countries enact war according to rules of engagement. We live by codes in all aspects of life.

Which values guide your organization? Is there a written Code of Ethics or a Code of Conduct? If you haven't already done so, it may be helpful to conduct a search for those documents and spend time becoming familiar with them. If you can't find online or paper documents, talk with the leadership within your organization. You may learn that there are handbooks, brochures, plaques on the wall, or other written communication that you didn't know existed but are important to your organization's culture.

MAKING SENSE OF NORMS AND CODES OF CONDUCT

In addition to understanding and abiding by your organization's formal and informal codes, a school leader must also know and follow the education code. It becomes challenging when you are faced with a situation that isn't reflected in existing laws and policies. Decision making becomes messy when laws are vague or contextual factors are not considered. Keep in mind, though, that the legal code is not a substitute for your conscience. We all know that it is possible to act unethically while still abiding by the law. Obeying the law is the minimum requirement; having high ethical standards and honorable conduct means adhering to basic values such as integrity, honesty, and equity as well as your commitment to upholding the collective vision of values and standards expected by your community and organization.

The position of principal can be lonely because in many cases there is no one at the site level with whom he or she can consult about a problem or seek guidance or feedback. For many principals, greater access to fellow principals and district-level leadership to answer questions, provide feedback, or simply act as a sounding board are necessary supports (Alvoid & Black, 2014).

ACTIVITY 2.3

Organization Values Audit

To find out what is important to your organization, collect information using these three probes:

What written codes, values, and expectations exist to guide employee performance? How are they measured?	
What programs and projects are valued by your organization? How do you know?	
What are the unspoken edicts of your organizational culture? Who might you need to talk to if you need more information?	

ACTIVITY 2.4

Organization Policy Analysis

Shaping a collective vision requires that leaders take steps to understand and investigate policies, procedures, and regulations on a regular basis.

What medical and dental services exist for students and families who don't have private insurance?	
What types of programs exist for Gifted and Talented students?	
Are students provided with transportation to and from school? If so, do all student groups have access to this service?	
What types of programs exist for English Learners?	
Does your district have any policies related to religion?	
Are religious organizations involved in schools or in the district?	
To what extent do employment and school enrollment policies include the range of gender demographics including male, female, intersex, transgender, and other?	
Are there written policies that address breast-feeding mothers in the workplace?	
What are the formal protocols for handling complaints from employees? From parents and the community?	
What organizational policies address sexual harassment? Gender identity? How are these communicated to employees?	
How does the organization address accommodations for employees with disabilities?	

STUDY COLLEAGUES' BEHAVIOR

Studying the actions of others and asking questions will help you to make sense of unwritten, but extremely important, policies. Once you have a solid understanding of the policies of your organization and community (both written and unwritten, formal and informal) you will be able to take steps to building a collective vision that improves the morale and quality of life for your community and that helps to nurture the optimal environment for your students.

Another structure worthy of investigation at the organizational level is the positional design of the system in which you work. Taking notice of the positions and titles of senior leadership provides you with additional insight into the values of the organization. Many districts have a director of curriculum, instruction, and assessment as well as a director in the human resources department. In addition to these standard positions, what other programs are valued by the district? Who oversees those? For instance, in my school district there is a full-time certificated manager of emergency operations and safety measures. This tells me that school safety is so important to my district and community that senior leadership and our school board willingly prioritize this position above other programs.

The People and Positions Appraisal found in Activity 2.5 involves gathering information about the organization from colleagues and senior leaders. Begin by establishing rapport with the individuals you wish to talk to—remember, this isn't an inquisition. Inquire from a place of curiosity, rather than judgment. Producing a list of questions may feel more like an interrogation, so instead, have some preplanned open-ended questions to ask. Not only do you learn the realities of your system, you also demonstrate an appetite to become more deeply connected to the organization.

ACTIVITY 2.5

People and Positions Appraisal

Does the organization have a Title IX administrator? If not, how are these issues addressed?	
How is school and organizational emergency preparedness handled? Who are the people assigned to manage student and school safety?	
Does the district have an English Learner coordinator? If not, what professional learning opportunities are provided to address these needs?	
Is there a Gifted and Talented Education director?	

The ethical challenge for the school principal is to resist the urge to impose his or her understanding of what's right and wrong to others, but instead seek to understand others' viewpoints. The power of one isn't enough anymore. To accomplish more with fewer resources, we must harness the collective energy of our community through cooperation and team spirit by listening generously (Strategy #3), creating an inclusive school climate side by side with others (Strategy #4), and by discovering your community's hopes and dreams and fulfilling those dreams as a team (Strategy #5). Collaborative leaders solicit feedback from all stakeholders to integrate core values and unify to jointly develop a shared vision.

The Reflective Questions that follow provide a space for you to note all of the information that you have gathered. It is important that you determine how all of the pieces fit together such that you are able to succinctly explain the values and perspectives of all stakeholders. A critical function of the leader is to unify the community and develop a detailed plan that leads to accomplishing the school vision.

Reflective Questions

Questions to Consider When Getting to Know the Values of Your School Community

- What values and practices are important to the community?
- What action steps is the community taking to reach the vision?
- What is the time line for reaching the vision?
- How is the organizational culture communicated to you and to others?
- What organizational values align with your personal values? Are there any incongruences? If so, what are they?
- How is the organizational culture communicated by you to others?

ADHERE TO ETHICAL AND LEGAL PARAMETERS

C hapters 1 and 2 asked readers to focus on individual, school, and community values. Chapter 3 takes on a broader view of ethical and equitable leadership in education by exploring the Professional Standards for Educational Leaders (PSEL). These standards were developed in 2015 and were adopted by the majority of states in the United States (Young & Perrone, 2016). They build upon and replace the Interstate School Leadership Consortium (ISLLC) Standards that existed for the previous 20 years (Murphy & Smylie, 2016).

While the PSELs were designed to drive practice, how they look in practice may vary because of local context, personal values, or community beliefs. This chapter covers the concepts of *easy ethics* and *messy ethics*. Easy ethics are the "no-brainer" decisions where right and wrong paths of action are straightforward and clear. Messy ethical decisions describe cases where decision makers are faced with right vs. right situations that pit one set of values against another. Decisions get messy when some groups of students are more advantaged than other groups of students. It's messy when some students receive fewer educational opportunities because of the color of their skin or their parents' income level. Strategy #7 asks principals to consider the moral and legal downstream consequences of the decisions they make. Acting ethically makes considering the moral and ethical aspects of these sensitive issues from multiple angles *before* making a decision. In this chapter you will find a framework for uncovering the ethical dimensions of problems to assist you in making decisions that are fair, just, and in the best interests of students. Strategy #8 asks leaders to reflect and take steps to ensure equitable processes and outcomes for *all* students. You will find a practical framework in the latter half of the chapter to help you in this endeavor.

PROFESSIONAL STANDARDS FOR EDUCATIONAL LEADERS

Principals, superintendents, and professional associations provided input into the development of the PSELs through focus groups and surveys. Educators collectively determined that the expectations of school leaders had changed significantly since 2008 (Wilson, 2017) such that previous standards were redesigned with a forward orientation that integrate the values and wisdom of professional practice with current research (Murphy & Smylie, 2016).

Since the responsibilities and expectations for school and district leaders evolve over time, so must the standards. The PSELs demonstrate that these standards are not static and are regularly reviewed and updated to reflect the profession's current context and expectations of leaders (Wilson, 2017). They apply to leaders at all levels in public school systems along the leadership continuum, from vice principals to superintendents. The standards are used by states, universities, districts, and schools as guidance for preparation, credentialing, practice, support, and evaluation (Young & Perrone, 2016).

A major change reflected in the PSELs is the greater emphasis on students, their learning, and the skills needed for successful entry into future jobs and careers. The PSELs emphasize that for learning to happen, educational leaders must focus all aspects of their work on students and student outcomes. While instructional pedagogy and curriculum are critical, they are not enough to prepare students to be skilled thinkers. As such, school leaders must approach every interaction, every teacher evaluation, and every analysis of data with one question in mind: *How will this help our students to excel as learners?* (National Policy Board for Educational Administration [NPBEA], 2015).

Since the PSELs are used to develop, support, and evaluate leaders at all levels (Frick, Bass, & Young, 2018), effective leaders should develop and maintain skillsets in the 10 identified domains:

Professional Standards for Educational Leaders

1. Mission, Vision, and Core Values
2. Ethics and Professional Norms
3. Equity and Cultural Responsiveness
4. Curriculum, Instruction, and Assessment
5. Community of Care and Support for Students
6. Professional Capacity of School Personnel
7. Professional Community for Teachers and Staff
8. Meaningful Engagement of Families and Community
9. Operations and Management
10. School Improvement

(NPBEA, 2015)

The 10 PSEL standards function as an interdependent system to promote each student's academic and social success. An important distinction between the ISLLC standards and the PSELs is that the ISLLC had grouped issues related to ethics, equity, and culturally responsive teaching together under a single domain, whereas the PSEL treat these as discreet topics, deserving of their own domains (Murphy, Louis, & Smylie, 2017). Additionally, educators elevated the status of Ethics and Professional Norms from Standard 5 in ISLLC to Standard 2 in PSEL, sending a clear message that "novice as well as experienced leaders need to take ethics very, very seriously" (Shapiro, 2018). This chapter will examine the importance and relevance of PSEL Standard 2 on Ethics and PSEL Standard 3 on Equity.

STRATEGY #7: CONSIDER MORAL AND LEGAL CONSEQUENCES OF DECISIONS

PSEL STANDARD 2: ETHICS AND PROFESSIONAL NORMS

Standard 2. Ethics and Professional Norms

Effective educational leaders act ethically and according to professional norms to promote *each* student's academic success and well-being.

Effective leaders:

a. Act ethically and professionally in personal conduct, relationships with others, decision-making, stewardship of the school's resources, and all aspects of school leadership.

b. Act according to and promote the professional norms of integrity, fairness, transparency, trust, collaboration, perseverance, learning, and continuous improvement.

c. Place children at the center of education and accept responsibility for each student's academic success and well-being.

d. Safeguard and promote the values of democracy, individual freedom and responsibility, equity, social justice, community, and diversity.

e. Lead with interpersonal and communication skill, social-emotional insight, and understanding of all students' and staff members' backgrounds and cultures.

f. Provide moral direction for the school and promote ethical and professional behavior among faculty and staff.

(NPBEA, 2015)

The prominent position of Ethics and Professional Norms within the PSEL (as the second domain, superseded only by Mission, Vision, and Core Values) indicates the critical import of an ethical approach to school leadership (Shapiro, 2018). Ethics must be the anchor of all practices as leaders work collectively with others to support quality instruction, promote a common vision, foster school improvement, and build a strong community committed to student learning (Frick et al., 2018; Young & Perrone, 2016).

The jobs of school leaders would be so much easier if standards, education laws, and district policies could be applied passively to resolve problems. Unfortunately, reality is much messier than theory. These standards are merely guideposts that signal the public's expectations regarding school governance. The job of the effective school leader is to interpret the standards and laws and determine how to best apply them to the complex, everyday dilemmas that arise in schools (NPBEA, 2015).

LEAD WITH MORAL COURAGE

The PSELs call greater attention to leading with a moral purpose. They recognize that educational leaders are responsible for placing vision, values, improvement, service, care, and ethics at the core of our daily work. In other words, we must put the common good above our own self-interests and the comfort of the adults in our schools and communities. The ability to adjust to the new and unique demands of today's world begins in our schools and requires that leaders have the courage to take stances that demonstrate commitment to the best interests of students, even if the stance is believed to be wrong by staff or parents. This is challenging because school leaders are left to decide for themselves when to uphold the community moral code or when to take a different course of action. Community input is desired, but it cannot be followed blindly. At the end of the day, responsible school leaders have to make decisions that adhere to their core values and remain true to their own Ethical Line. This requires moral courage.

While moral courage is necessary to lead in today's times, it is also necessary to consider the school context. It makes a difference whether a school is in a remote setting, a suburban area, or in an urban environment. Leaders must also consider whether students come from advantaged or disadvantaged homes, and whether immigrant or refugee children have had opportunities to attend school in their countries of origin. Additionally, school leaders must be able to determine general standards of conduct that are universally applicable, even if they are implemented differently across different contexts.

Leaders who demonstrate moral courage must also jointly negotiate criteria that promotes equity for all members of the community, as opposed to simply identifying approaches that make the organization, in the aggregate, look successful. If disaggregating the data of marginalized student populations shows lack of success for those targeted groups, then the policy and strategy of the whole school needs to be adjusted to ensure the success of all students—from the marginalized to the privileged. Making these decisions may result in quite a bit of backlash and criticism from powerful groups in the community. Therefore, leading with moral courage means taking steps to motivate the disgruntled factions to work collaboratively toward raising the learning achievement of all students.

Be Mindful of Downstream Consequences

Everyone makes mistakes, and principals are no exception. However, when a principal makes a mistake, the outcome can have consequences that significantly affect a wide range of people—and to make things worse, that mistake will likely be discussed and critiqued in a very public way. PSEL Standard 2 requires educational leaders to use ethics and professional norms in all aspects of leadership. I learned about (what I'm calling) *The Case of the Soiled School Spirit* from a colleague of mine who works in that school district. As you read the case, take notice of the principal's intent to generate school spirit but also notice the consequences that resulted from her failure to consult the proper channels and consider all possible outcomes.

THE CASE OF THE SOILED SCHOOL SPIRIT

High School Principal
Southern California

Consider this true story: An experienced, well-intentioned principal brainstormed ways to enliven school spirit on her high school campus. She decided to create a berm on the football field where the school's logo could be placed.

The principal thought this was a good idea as all of the students used the field at various times for PE and many attended Friday night football games. She located the 12,000 tons of dirt on Craig's List and arranged for it to be dumped on one side of the field. Before the dirt could be packed down and molded into letters, a small dust storm kicked up. Concerned parents worried that their children would inhale the dirt during athletic activities. More parent complaints ensued, leading the district to contract with an outside agency who confirmed that the dirt contained low levels of lead and pesticides. The school community (and district leaders) were furious about the dirt debacle and the fact that they hadn't been consulted about the project. The dirt ended up sitting on the field for over a year while investigations continued. In the end, it took 485 truckloads to remove the dirt, costing the district an estimated $500,000 (Dipping, 2012).

It is likely that some readers will sympathize with this principal. Although ill-conceived, the intention was to enhance school spirit. There was no malice or ill will, but she made a big blunder by not getting approval from the school district. Had she consulted with someone, she might have decided not to purchase the tainted dirt. As it was, dangerous chemicals were introduced onto the school field under her watch and based on her directive. While the intent was good, the effect was that students' health was compromised. The district was forced to pay a significant sum to clean up the mess.

The Case of the Soiled School Spirit illustrates a principal's failure to consider the downstream consequences of her actions. She is guilty of not being aware of her blind spots. The blind spot in this example is that she underestimated the extremes: she didn't consider potential problems that could arise from procuring dirt from an unknown source. Her lack of judgment in this case calls attention to the first responsibility of every school principal: to protect the safety and well-being of students, the school, and the organization.

It appears that the principal's decision regarding where to purchase the dirt was made in isolation. Collaborating with others demonstrates distributive leadership, builds agency, and fosters ownership such that these blunders are less likely to happen. When relied upon, our community members can probe our thinking and potentially illuminate unseen blind spots. Consulting others before acting can conceivably save you from making poor decisions that jeopardize students' safety or your own career.

Beware of Decision Traps

Making decisions is an essential function of the principalship. However, making decisions can be time-consuming, risky, and often causes people stress. Poor decision making may harm your students, families, organizations, and ultimately your career, sometimes irreparably. So where do poor decisions come from? In many cases, they can be linked to how the problem was initially approached. Reflect on a recent thorny situation that you were involved in. To learn and grow from the situation, it may be helpful to look back and recall your state of mind before you made your final decision. How would you have answered the questions in the Tool 3.1 Decision-Trap Checklist at that time?

TOOL 3.1

Decision-Trap Checklist

- ☐ Have you gathered enough information?
- ☐ Is the information you gathered accurate? How do you know? Did you triangulate by consulting various sources?
- ☐ Have you considered alternative theories and solutions? Should you spend more time doing this?
- ☐ Have you consulted with trusted colleagues and team members to brainstorm solutions and reality-check your thinking?
- ☐ Are you allowing outside influences to pressure you into making a hasty decision?
- ☐ Are your own personal biases clouding your judgment? What steps can you take to make sure this isn't the case?
- ☐ Are your emotions clouding your judgment? Do you need to step away for a bit to calm down and regroup?
- ☐ Have you considered the most likely positive and negative outcomes of your decision? (Spend some time considering the unlikely outcomes as well.)
- ☐ Have you taken steps to ensure buy-in from community members—will they support your decision? If not, what steps can you take to earn their support?
- ☐ Refer back to the A–F descriptors of effective principals outlined in PSEL 2: Ethics and Professional Norms. Has your decision-making process and subsequent decision followed the spirit and essence of those descriptors? If not, what steps can you take to make sure that you are reflecting the norms outlined in PSEL 2?

To ensure that our biases are not clouding our judgment, it is usually a good idea to consult others and use trusted colleagues and team members as sounding boards. "Imperfections in decision making occur when biases distort the decision-maker's ability to apply objective or logical thinking" (Davis, 2005). Biases can occur in several ways, including using incomplete or one-sided thinking, relying on our personal preferences, being influenced by others, or when our motives are self-serving and not in the best interests of students. When we're not mindful of these biases, we may make mistakes from the onset of the problem and throughout the decision-making process.

Our mental state also impacts our problem-solving abilities. Most of us are taught to make decisions with a cool head; we've all had experience with making a rash decision "in the moment" based upon a prevailing emotion of anger, fear, desire, or other unsteady state of mind. The more we understand the factors that impact our decisions, the better we can manage them.

Before deciding on a course of action, skillful decision makers evaluate the situation before them and consider all perspectives. Unfortunately, some people are overly cautious and become plagued with analysis paralysis—and they don't act. Others are overconfident—they underestimate possible negative outcomes. And still others are wishy-washy. Since they are unsure, they vacillate between potential solutions.

When we are ensnared in decision traps we often have no awareness that we've fallen prey to the trap. Decision traps are sneaky; they catch even the best decision makers. When facing a particularly thorny and emotion-triggering decision, use the checklist provided in Tool 3.1 to stop and assess whether you are letting unhelpful thinking cloud your judgment. How might *The Case of the Soiled School Spirit* have turned out differently if the principal had consulted the Tool 3.1 checklist before making a decision to purchase the dirt (and where to purchase it from)?

A FRAMEWORK FOR MAKING
ETHICAL DECISIONS

In additional to the reflection questions listed in Tool 3.1, another way to approach ethical decision making is to use the framework outlined by Shapiro and Stefkovich (2016). The four-pronged framework, which Shapiro and Stefkovich call the *Multiple Ethical Paradigms*, can be applied to analyze and classify decisions made by educational leaders.

These paradigms, or mindsets, are *the Ethic of Justice, the Ethic of Care*, *the Ethic of Critique*, and *the Ethic of the Profession*. One person may lean toward one particular paradigm over the others. For example, a principal who professes the benefits of restorative practices may be more inclined to apply the Ethic of Care to moral dilemmas rather than the Ethic of Justice.

Though it has been argued that school leaders can and should use these ethical lenses simultaneously (Eyal, Berkovich, & Schwartz, 2010), they can be discussed individually to break down the reasoning behind the decisions principals make in their schools (Shapiro & Stefkovich, 2016).

Multiple Ethical Paradigms

Try using these mindsets to classify your responses to situations that arise in your work. Which of these ethical paradigms most appeals to your personal style? Can you see the benefit of the other paradigms? How might the quality of your decisions improve if you tried to apply all (or a combination) of the paradigms together?

The Ethic of Justice

Justice is the foundation for legal principles and ideals, rights and laws, and fairness and equity in individual freedom. The Ethic of Justice mindset maintains that people are held to a certain standard of justice in all situations. The idea of fairness and equal treatment are the core values of the Ethic of Justice. This approach supports the notion of due process to protect the civil and human rights of all people. The Ethic of Justice promotes maximum good to the majority of people, regardless of harm to specific individuals.

In school settings, the Ethic of Justice is demonstrated by one's commitment to equality of opportunities. Case in point: Elijah is a 7-year-old boy who was caught stealing food from the school cafeteria. A principal who applies the Ethic of Justice would adhere to the school policy that states that Elijah should be suspended for

(Continued)

(Continued)

stealing. This ethic operates under the belief that all students have the opportunity to behave according to the established norms, and any who violate those norms will receive the predetermined punishment. Justice is blind, fair, and equally applied to all. This ethic protects the rights of the group from theft.

The Ethic of Care

The second mindset, the Ethic of Care, emphasizes compassion and empathy. This approach promotes caring for individuals as unique persons. It is the ideal fulfillment of all social relationships. When this approach is promoted in school settings, principals value relationships and connections when making decisions, rather than relying on rigid rules. It is responsive to an individual's distress. Educators who act with an Ethic of Care mindset put students at the center of all decision making.

An Ethic of Care can be seen when context-specific information is utilized to inform a decision. Typically, questions are asked that illuminate the reason why the act occurred. *"Why did Elijah steal food from the cafeteria? Was he hungry? Does he not get enough food? What's going on in Elijah's home? Was stealing a cry for attention? How can we help Elijah and his family?"* Elijah is counseled to ask for help (and food) when he needs it.

The Ethic of Critique

The Ethic of Critique is concerned with challenging the status quo and encouraging voices from marginalized populations. Proponents of this approach push leaders to not only reconsider laws and justice but also to rethink constructs such as power, privilege, language, and culture. The Ethic of Critique relates to the obstruction of fairness and is demonstrated when educators seek to change rules, policies, and laws that disproportionally benefit some groups in society and fail others.

An Ethic of Critique is demonstrated when someone advocates for changing a rule or policy. In this case, school personnel would address the policy of stealing. Does the policy apply to students who steal food when they are hungry? Why does the "system" get to decide when and what Elijah eats? Should the policy about stealing be confined to malicious intent? A principal applying the Ethic of Critique might suggest that Elijah should feel empowered to take what he needs to overcome the oppressive systems controlling him and/or keeping him hungry.

The Ethic of the Profession

This mindset studies the Ethics of Justice, Care, and Critique, but it also considers the expectations of the profession, what happens when personal and professional ethics collide, and how school leaders' ethical decision making is influenced by the community. When a dilemma is viewed through all lenses, the Ethic of the Profession emerges. Using this approach, school leaders reflect on their personal and professional values to formulate a response that focuses on the best interests of students.

In Elijah's case, an Ethic of the Profession is demonstrated when the educators contact Elijah's parents to work together toward an appropriate outcome for him. Stealing isn't OK, therefore he will face a sensible consequence to help Elijah learn from this experience.

THE SEVEN STEPS OF ETHICAL DECISION MAKING

PSEL 2 outlines criteria for ethical and effective school leaders. In line with those criteria, the decision-making process of ethical school leaders should be organized around two central tenets: (1) the decision is ethically sound and (2) the decision aligns to the school, district, and community values. For another guideline in this endeavor, consider the PLUS Ethical Decision Making Model outlined by the Ethics and Compliance Initiative (2019b). It offers seven key steps for making fair and equitable decisions.

TOOL 3.2

The PLUS Ethical Decision Making Model

Step 1: Identify and frame the problem. How you frame the problem has a profound effect on whether or not your investigation accurately leads to the heart of the matter. During this step, you determine the primary challenge and factors that are contributing to the problem. It is important that you explore the difference between the current reality and your expectations. By framing the problem in terms of outcomes, you can clearly state the problem.

Step 2: Gather information and seek guidance from others. Once you have framed the issue, it is crucial to seek resources to aid you in making a good decision. Resources may include people (i.e., colleagues, mentors, external experts) as well as professional guidelines such as organizational policies or regulations. These resources are vital in the process of determining parameters and developing solutions.

Step 3: Identify new feasible solutions to the problem. The key to this step is to look beyond the obvious choices and to not rely upon a solution that has worked in the past. Consider new and better alternatives; aim to identify three to five possible solutions so that you don't limit your alternatives to two opposing choices. Identifying multiple solutions also forces you to see all sides of the issue.

Step 4: Evaluate the alternatives. After you have identified three to five potential solutions, determine the positive and negative consequences of each solution. Be careful to differentiate between what you know as a fact and what you believe to be the case. Although you will supplement the facts with informed beliefs and realistic assumptions, keeping your evaluation fact-based will increase the chances of reaching your expected outcome.

Step 5: Make the decision. It is important to note that enacting the decision looks different for individuals than when working with a team. When working with a team you'll need to make a proposal that includes a clear definition of the problem, a list of the alternatives that were considered by the team, and a clear rationale (developed by the team) for the mutually agreed-upon solution.

Step 6: Implement the decision. While this may seem obvious to some, it is necessary to point out that selecting the best solution is not the same as implementing it. Acting upon the decision is the first real and tangible step to improving the situation.

Step 7: Evaluate the impact of the decision. Every decision is based upon fixing a problem. The final component of this process is to determine whether the problem was partially or completely fixed. Did the solution improve the situation substantially? Did any new problems arise as a result of the solution? Take a few moments to reflect on what you learned from this experience. Note that failing to reflect is failing to learn.

The Seven Steps of Ethical Decision Making is a useful approach that ensures all angles of a problem and its solution are considered. When we are intentional and thorough, we uphold the tenets of PSEL 2 on Ethics and Integrity.

Ethical Lenses

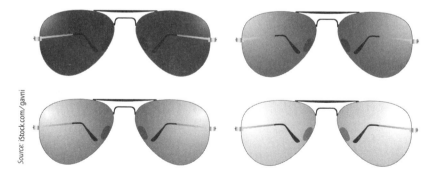

Source: iStock.com/gavni

I like to think of the ethical components of the decision-making process as a set of lenses (or what the Ethics and Compliance Initiative [2019a] calls "filters") through which we can view an issue. The purpose of the lenses is to illustrate how we can view the same problem differently, depending on the context and the individuals involved. During each of the seven steps of ethical decision making, it is recommended that you apply the four PLUS filters. By examining the issue from these viewpoints, you can expose the ethical dimensions of the problem.

The Ethics and Compliance Initiative has organized the lenses into an easy-to-remember mnemonic (PLUS) that reminds us of our ethical obligations when evaluating decisions we have made:

- **P** = Policies. *Is this decision consistent with my organization's policies, procedures, and guidelines?*
- **L** = Legal. *Is this solution acceptable under the applicable laws and regulations?*
- **U** = Universal. *Does this course of action conform to the universal principles/values my organization has adopted?*
- **S** = Self. *Does this solution satisfy my personal definition of right, good, and fair?*

(Ethics and Compliance Initiative, 2019a)

Applying these lenses will help you to identify the ethical component(s) of the issue and whether or not they are being addressed in your decision. They don't guarantee an ethically sound decision, but applying them ensures that ethically sensitive elements of the issue are considered.

As you read about *The Case of the Differentiated Discipline*, think about how this situation might have played out differently had Principal Cho applied the seven steps of ethical decision making when she determined consequences for a student who broke playground rules.

THE CASE OF THE DIFFERENTIATED DISCIPLINE

Principal Cho
Elementary School
California

Ms. Cho (a pseudonym) was the principal of a high-performing elementary school in an affluent neighborhood. She frequently stated that she based her decisions on fairness, equity, and the success of students. However, her actions didn't match what she said. A fourth-grader (let's call him Stuart) often displayed challenging behavior and bullied other children. Stuart started fights with new students, stole lunches, and often excluded other children from playing games at recess. Stuart was the son of a school board member. Because of his behavior, Stuart was often sent to Principal Cho's office to receive consequences for his infractions. However, it appeared to other parents, students, and staff that Principal Cho was being overly lenient regarding Stuart's behavior in consideration of his father's position on the school board. Many parents and teachers voiced concerns to Principal Cho about her lack of consistency and lack of fairness in meting out consequences to all students equally, but she ignored their complaints and often stated, *"I am the principal, and I always do what's best on behalf of our children."*

Unlike Stuart, when other students initiated fights, they received in-school or out-of-school suspensions and were removed from the playground for a week depending on the offense. But, when Stuart initiated a fight, he would have to sit out for five minutes and would then be allowed to return to the playground only to cause more mischief. Stuart would often be caught laughing and bragging, *"I run this school. My dad is on the school board. I can do what I want."* This infuriated the teachers, playground supervisors, and other students.

One day, Stuart pulled the hair of a new student for no reason at all. Per usual, Principal Cho had him take a five-minute time-out during recess. But, this time, the teachers were angry and decided that a five-minute time-out was not a suitable consequence. So, they informed other fourth-grade parents about the incident and urged the parents to start a petition and present it to the superintendent. Later, a group of parents attended the next School Site Council meeting and shared that they did not trust Principal Cho's ability to make ethical decisions. They shared that they felt a "good principal" should be a role model of fairness. Principal Cho was forced to apologize and agreed to make more equitable decisions in the future.

One approach to resolving *The Case of the Differentiated Discipline* might have been for Principal Cho, the teachers, parents, and playground staff to create an inclusive student discipline committee with the aim of developing a behavior management and discipline rubric to ensure that all students received appropriate and consistent rewards and consequences for their actions. This joint collaboration would allow each stakeholder group to share their concerns and desires as the ideas were presented and agreed upon. Once the group developed a framework to increase desired student behavior, they could share the draft and the committee goals with the larger community, inviting them to provide additional input. The goal would be to foster inclusivity, shared goals, and deepen trust among the different stakeholder groups. Figure 3.1 describes a possible course of action based upon the Seven Steps of Ethical Decision Making.

Figure 3.1   Treating Students Equitably

Steps	PLUS	*What could Principal Cho have done better?*
Step 1: **Define the problem using facts (consult PLUS filters)**	**P:** What is the student behavior **policy** at this school? **L:** What **laws** apply to this situation? **U:** Does my decision align with the **universal** standards of my school and district? **S:** Does my decision align with my own **self-identified** core values?	Fact: Stuart is the son of a school board member. Fact: Stuart's consequences are inconsistent with the consequences meted out to other students for the same or similar behavior. Fact: Stuart's behavior continues to be a chronic problem over time. The consequences he receives are not proving to be a deterrent and they are not improving his behavior.
Step 2: **Seek out relevant information, assistance, guidance, and support**		Principal Cho could have asked herself: ■ Have I consulted with my colleagues, teachers, mentors, or external experts? What was their advice? ■ Have I considered the professional guidelines such as organizational policies or regulations? What actions would they advocate for in this situation?

Steps	PLUS	*What could Principal Cho have done better?*
		■ What are the discipline trends at our school? ■ How do other schools and systems handle similar student behavior? ■ What are local, state, and national trends and directives toward equitable discipline?
Step 3: **Identify alternatives**		Principal Cho could have resisted the urge to be lenient with Stuart as she had in the past. Principal Cho could have formed a discipline committee made up of teachers, staff, and student leaders. She could have asked the committee to identify multiple solutions to examine all sides of the issue. Principal Cho could have asked herself if there were gender or racial differences contributing to the discipline problem. What factors could she have considered to come up with an assessment?
Step 4: **Evaluate the alternatives (consult PLUS filters)**	Policy: What is the policy? Legal: Is the consequence justifiable? Universal: How are students held accountable to the policy? Self: Am I OK with giving preferential treatment to one student?	Principal Cho could have asked herself: What are the positive and negative consequences of ■ being lenient with Stuart? ■ treating Stuart differently from other students? ■ treating all students the same? ■ holding Stuart accountable for his actions? ■ increasing the number of playground supervisors? ■ reinforcing positive behaviors? ■ offering additional training to playground supervisors to prevent these problems from recurring? What will training look like?

(Continued)

Figure 3.1 (Continued)

Steps	PLUS	*What could Principal Cho have done better?*
Step 5: **Make the decision**		Principal Cho might have decided to: ■ provide communication to the staff and school community that explains the problem and the solution. ■ ensure that all stakeholders understand the behavior issues. ■ articulate the group thinking that evolved as the committee discussed how to improve behavior at the school.
Step 6: **Implement the decision**		Principal Cho could have ■ implemented a system of behavior modification and supervision. ■ monitored the effectiveness of the systems quarterly and followed up with communication to staff and the school community regarding progress, reassessment, and trouble-shooting efforts.
Step 7: **Evaluate the decision (consult PLUS filters)**	Policy: Is the policy working as written or does it need to be amended? Self: Have you checked in with staff and students to gauge their understanding and agreement with the policy?	Principal Cho could ask herself: ■ How are you measuring success? ■ Did the behavior infractions decrease substantially? ■ Did any new problems arise as a result of the solution? She could then reconvene the group on a monthly basis to review and discuss the data and any unforeseen consequences.

The Case of the Differentiated Discipline provides an example of an occasion when a principal did not take important, ethical considerations into account before making a decision. The norms that PSEL 2 outlines for effective and ethical leadership require that leaders make decisions responsibly. Following the steps outlined in the PLUS Ethical Decision Making Model can help school leaders predict potential consequences of decisions before implementing them.

Easy Ethics

School board policies, administrative regulations, and education codes exist to provide school districts and educational organizations with a framework of laws to guide us. These policies govern many of the tasks and the personnel who are employed to educate and care for students. They provide legal direction to most aspects of the educational processes in public schools. If there's a policy that applies to your situation, and you follow it to a tee, that's an easy decision, or easy ethics. Easy ethics require less thought because the situation is straightforward and uncomplicated.

Thousands of national and state policies exist. The U.S. Department of Education is a federal organization that directs and oversees national directives, while each state elects a State Board of Education which directs and oversees the academic standards, curriculum, assessments, instructional materials, and accountability of the schools and districts within each state. Typically, each state uses a standardized numbering process to organize its policies. Each local education agency refines and details them to provide guidance to their respective organizations. There may be some variance depending on what is expected and valued in each region, though ultimately these policies drive the functions of each district and its organizational culture. Having these policies in place, knowing what they are, and making the effort to follow them makes the work of a harried school leader much, much easier.

Unfortunately, situations aren't always simple. In some situations, school leaders might find that the prescribed solution does not fit the needs and circumstances of the problem at hand. Or you might look at the law and see that it can be interpreted in various and contrasting ways. The policy might not apply to the extenuating factors. Circumstances might become complicated by the people involved or those who have the final say. What makes sense in one school community may not make sense in a neighboring community. There are many situations that necessitate making an exception to the rule. The policy might not cover all of the "what-ifs" that are raised when you carefully analyze the problem. You might also find that adhering to the policy in a given situation would lead to an injustice being done to a student or a group of students; following the law or policy might lead to a violation of your core values. In these cases, you're facing a case of messy ethics. As an effective and ethical leader, it is important to carefully assess each situation to evaluate whether it is a case of easy ethics or messy ethics.

Messy Ethics

The term "messy" in this sense is not meant to carry a negative connotation. Rather, here messy refers to the complicated situations and dilemmas that cannot be adequately resolved by solely adhering to one policy without consideration of the context and other related factors. Decisions that are messy often occur when there is not a clear answer; the solution is somewhere in the gray area. In some ethical dilemmas, there may not be a single right or a wrong response; the options may be "right or right."

Ethical dilemmas arise in school settings when principals face delicate circumstances that require them to choose from competing sets of principles, values, beliefs, or ideals. These messy problems are often people-centered and have political or professional undertones. Principals must maintain their Ethical Lines while simultaneously accessing their mental toolboxes to consider their own beliefs and inherent biases, contemplate the different aspects of the problem, and sometimes make difficult moral choices.

There is considerable evidence that suggests that there is greater immediacy and complexity in the field of educational administration that was not experienced by principals in the past (Hull, 2018). There are two explanations for this: first, the nature and degree of change in society has caused some people to feel less certain about their lives and their futures; and second, public engagement has altered the ways schools are now managed and many issues find their way onto school grounds. Some of the societal changes impacting the ways schools function include racism and religious fundamentalism, harassment, gender inequity, sexuality, violence, differing family structures, child abuse, information and communication technology, health and well-being, and the litigious nature of Western society. Our schools are replete with complicated situations. In other words, we have a lot of messy ethics on our hands.

From an outsider's point of view, adhering to policies may seem like *"the right thing to do."* However, when acting in the best interests of children, sometimes "the law is wrong" (Stefkovich, 2014, p. 33) or it is unclear. The judicial system has limitations. However, you can make your role as an ethical leader easier by ensuring that the decisions you make are in the best interest of a child or group of children. You'll also need to justify the decision you chose to make to your stakeholders, explaining the reasoning as to why you strayed from codified policy. Chapter 1 provided activities to uncover your core values in order to understand your Ethical Line. As you read *The Case of Nate's Knife*, consider if this situation would cause you to challenge existing rules by utilizing the Ethic of Critique or the Ethic of Justice.

THE CASE OF NATE'S KNIFE

Nate, First-grader
Elementary School
Anywhere, USA

One of those messy ethics dilemmas can occur when a student brings a knife to school. These cases are controversial and often bring media attention. Education code and local policies may contain zero-tolerance rules regarding the disciplinary consequence when a student has violated the no-weapon rule. However, as a principal, how would you respond if a 6-year-old child (we'll call him Nate) brought a butter knife to school because he needed it to cut his sandwich at lunch? As there was no intent to harm himself or others, and no one ended up getting hurt, what would be the most ethical response? Would the ethical response be to follow the school policy and suspend Nate, or would a more ethical response be to use the incident as a teachable moment for Nate and other students? In this case, would it be unethical to violate the school policy by not suspending Nate? This is a situation where people, intent, lack of understanding, and circumstances make seemingly cut-and-dry policies messy and complex.

- What are the repercussions for the principal who ignores board policy and doesn't suspend Nate?
- What is the message to other students, families, and staff that a child violated the zero-tolerance policy and "got away with it"?
- Does this action give the green light to other children who conclude that they can bring weapons to school without fear of punishment?
- Does the age and maturity level of the child matter?
- Does the time of day the knife was discovered matter?
- Has there been a documented history of violence on the part of the child?
- What if another child found the knife and hurt someone?
- What if Nate had reached into his lunchbox and injured himself?
- Should a 6-year-old boy have permanent records in his cumulative file that state he was suspended for bringing a knife to school?

The fact that the situation prompted all of these questions indicates that there is no easy path toward a simple solution. Some people will argue that zero tolerance means zero tolerance, while others may contend that this is a teachable moment for Nate and the school. This example, and many others like it, demonstrate that making decisions in a school environment is not as simple as we might like it to be.

The investigation of an incident, the downstream consequences of a decision, public opinion, and pressure from different sources all complicate the decision-making process. In short, principals cannot make mechanistic decisions because dealing with people is complicated. Because the field of education is truly a human development endeavor, dealing with people gets messy. Let's look at two different decision pathways in Figure 3.2 using the PLUS (Policy, Legal, Universal, Self) lenses to determine how these responses might play out.

Figure 3.2   Which Response Resonates Most With Your Core Values?

Ethic of Justice: To Suspend	Ethic of Care: Not to Suspend
Policy: A zero-tolerance policy is enforced without exception. If exceptions are made, there is no point in having a policy because people will justify reasons for exceptions.	**Policy:** The zero-tolerance policy does not apply to this situation because of: ■ the child's age (6) ■ lack of intent to harm ■ the fact that no one was hurt
Legal: Because of his age and lack of intent, it is unlikely that the child has broken the law. Penal Code and Education Code deem that children under a certain age (typically 14) don't have a true understanding of committing a crime.	**Legal:** A 6-year-old child may have a general understanding of the difference between right and wrong but is not a criminal.
Universal: The values of the community promote the best interest of the child and what the child could learn from this situation. Nate's community would likely not support the idea of suspension.	**Universal:** Other educators would likely agree that the decision not to suspend is preferable because of the age of the child. There is less harm to the child. Inflicting a harsh punishment only for the sake of following a rule may not be meaningful to Nate.
Self: By making the determination to suspend, is the principal following his or her Ethical Line that says what is good, right, and fair?	**Self:** By making the determination not to suspend, is the principal following his or her Ethical Line that says what is good, right, and fair?

The dilemma of whether Nate should be suspended for bringing a knife to school may be an easy decision for some, while it is perplexing for others who view the situation as a teachable moment and one where the needs of the child should take precedence over the need to blindly follow a rule. That's the nature of a dilemma: there are context-specific factors that complicate the decision-making process.

If your decision tree doesn't include consideration of the PLUS lenses, you might find yourself adhering to your Ethical Line but disregarding the principles of your district or organization. You might feel good about sticking to your own core values, but you risk negative consequences by not foreseeing all possible reactions and fallout.

When you do decide to break with established policy, use the PLUS lenses (or an equally thorough reflection exercise) and be prepared to justify your actions and decisions to your boss, your organization, and your community. Explaining your decision and the reasoning behind it will make the situation a teachable moment not just for Nate but for the whole school and community as well. Make a practice of *explicitly* leading ethically—in your parent and staff meetings, in your newsletter, by explicitly stating your own personal core values, your ethical duties, the school's disciplinary policies, and the shared values that guide your decision making. Sharing your thinking publicly will go a long way to establishing your credibility as an effective and ethical leader and will help earn the trust of your community.

Constructively Challenge the Status Quo

The previous example about whether or not to suspend 6-year-old Nate for bringing a knife to school is an example of a principal challenging the status quo in a constructive way. In choosing to violate the zero-tolerance policy, the principal must come to terms with that decision and its repercussions. This type of decision demonstrates courageous leadership. It's critical that the principal communicates her reasoning for the decision while simultaneously protecting Nate's reputation and right to privacy.

If, on the other hand, the principal chooses to suspend Nate in accordance to her organization's policy, she would be satisfying (at least) three of the four ethics lenses: Legal, Policy, and Universal, and perhaps also the fourth, Self, since the decision to suspend may resonate with her own core values.

It's okay, and sometimes necessary, to lean off of your organization's Ethical Line, or perhaps even take a small step, in order to see the greater good and perhaps even enact a necessary change in service of a child's or group's needs. Leading ethically by stepping off of your organization's Ethical Line for a moment is a conscious and constructive attempt to make things better by questioning and challenging existing policies and laws to ask if they are ethical, and if not, do they need to be changed or discarded? Certain occasions warrant this pause and moment of critical analysis. We need to acknowledge and recognize that there are some policies and procedures that privilege certain groups over others. When we come to that realization, change may be needed, and even lawful. Take this step carefully and anticipate possible reactions. A step off of your organization's Ethical Line, or going against the grain, may be necessary, but it is usually uncomfortable.

STRATEGY #8: ENSURE EQUITABLE PROCESSES AND OUTCOMES

When you step off of your organization's ethical line, you are taking a risk. Sometimes there is justification for the risk, as in the case of 6-year-old Nate bringing a knife to school. Most principals who would make the decision not to suspend would feel the need to explain the "why" behind the decision. They are prepared to defend the decision because it makes sense, given the circumstances. An ethical dilemma may do just that: compel you to disregard a policy because a better alternative exists. But anytime you go against the grain, it's usually difficult. You may feel doubt or angst; there's a tension when you deviate from your organization's Ethical Line. While taking this stand might be the ethical thing to do, you have to be prepared for it. If you rock the boat, be ready for some rough water.

Typically, we feel secure when our Ethical Line matches that of our organization: it's steady and there's no fear. Your sense of self feels balanced. Courageous decisions are infrequent. Most of the time, you should be walking in sync with your organization's Ethical Line. If you find yourself stepping off habitually, something may be wrong. Finding a trusted colleague to share your thoughts and concerns with would be a good idea for processing your thoughts and checking to make sure that your reasoning is valid or if perhaps you need to get back to your Ethical Line. It might also be the case that there are structural problems within your organization that need to be addressed.

If you have chosen to constructively challenge the status quo in service of student learning or well-being, good for you! The Professional Standards for Educational Leaders (PSELs) urge us to make every effort to ensure students are provided with an education that is founded on democratic ideals and equitable practices.

PSEL STANDARD 3: ADVOCATE FOR ALL

Standard 3: Equity and Cultural Responsiveness

Effective educational leaders strive for equity of educational opportunity and culturally responsive practices to promote *each* student's academic success and well-being.

Effective leaders:

a. Ensure that each student is treated fairly, respectfully, and with an understanding of each student's culture and context.

b. Recognize, respect, and employ each student's strengths, diversity, and culture as assets for teaching and learning.

c. Ensure that each student has equitable access to effective teachers, learning opportunities, academic and social support, and other resources necessary for success.

d. Develop student policies and address student misconduct in a positive, fair, and unbiased manner.

e. Confront and alter institutional biases of student marginalization, deficit-based schooling, and low expectations associated with race, class, culture and language, gender and sexual orientation, and disability or special status.

f. Promote the preparation of students to live productively in and contribute to the diverse cultural contexts of a global society.

g. Act with cultural competence and responsiveness in their interactions, decision making, and practice.

h. Address matters of equity and cultural responsiveness in all aspects of leadership.

PSEL Standard 3 highlights the diversity across the United States and acknowledges that inequities exist in schools and communities. Whereas the previous standards called for civic mindedness, PSEL 3—specifically item (e)—directly addresses the promotion of educational equity and social justice in a democratic society. Is it possible to be an ethical leader if you deny that inequities between groups of students don't exist? Having an orientation toward nondiscriminatory practices is specifically called out in the standards. This section states that educational leaders are charged with confronting and altering institutional biases that marginalize students (NPBEA, 2015).

Principals are tasked with using quantitative and qualitative data to identify the inequities at their school sites. We are expected to remove any barriers to high-quality education that derive from economic, cultural, social, gender, language, physical, or other cause of discrimination and disadvantage. Further, we must work collaboratively with members of the school community to allocate funds and resources in equitable ways that support students' diverse needs. Ethical leaders must be the advocates for equity in their communities, districts, and states.

Confront Discriminatory Policies

Another responsibility of ethical leaders is to ensure that students who are already struggling in school settings are not further disadvantaged by school policies and practices. In the current educational landscape of high-stakes testing, equity in schools is more important than ever. Shared decision making is crucial, but ultimately the principal is responsible for the positive and negative consequences of programs, curriculum, and pedagogy. Today's principals must be well-informed, have the ability to understand and negotiate complex policies, and operate in ways that are transparent and inclusive. Ethical principals must enact and guide bias-free procedures and orchestrate a number of complex practices while preventing potential harm to students, staff, and communities that may result from inequitable or ineffective decisions.

Become an Equity-Driven Leader

In some cases, especially those involving equity, our perspectives might evolve following a realization that a policy needs to be revised. After this realization, your ethic of critique will be on high alert and you will feel compelled to reconcile issues of bias, bigotry, racism, or classism among many others. When this happens, identify strategies to help you promote equitable processes and outcomes in the organization in which you work. The Educational Leadership Department at San Diego State University, where I am a faculty member, developed a definition of equity that highlights these concerns.

Equity

- **Recognizes** that every student comes to school with a unique identity profile that is too often impacted by racism, bias, or bigotry.
- **Occurs** as a result of sensitive, courageous, and creative conversations and actions.
- **Requires** the distribution and redistribution of resources and initiatives based on individual and group needs derived from multiple sources of qualitative and quantitative data.
- **Leads** to engaged, inspired, and successful learners.

Each leader must rely on his or her own Ethical Line to make decisions that advance equitable processes and promote equitable outcomes for students. The field of education needs courageous leaders who advocate for children and who are champions for equity. The traditional school model was constructed for an earlier, less diverse population that wasn't saddled with today's problems. Principals in today's schools are positioned to be ethical leaders who identify inequitable practices, enact change when necessary, and use an adaptive leadership approach to mobilize school community members in the effort to ensure equity for all students.

Being an equity-driven leader means going against the grain and fighting for policy changes. It means questioning the ethicality of rules and procedures that were written without taking into account the diverse needs of the changing student population. Remember that you have been honored with a mandate to serve and nurture *all* students to reach their full potential.

An assessment of qualitative and quantitative information is needed to create the specific conditions necessary for all students to reach their full potentials. This may include the reallocation of fiscal and human resources that were previously used differently. It's important to go back to your data and work with your leadership teams to identify the most prudent uses of resources for the students you are serving today. For example, if language arts scores show that groups of students need additional language support to be successful in all curricular areas, how might the master schedule be adapted to maximize language acquisition? How might teachers in all content areas provide relevant, standards-aligned learning tasks that meet students where they are? How might interventions be structured so that no students fall through the cracks?

SUMMARY

School districts create guidelines and shared value statements so that each employee, independent of position or level, understands the expectations. Following these guidelines ensures that people feel confident and empowered that they are making sound decisions and acting within established protocols. However, if you find that following established policies does not align with your internal moral compass, it may be because the system needs to be challenged to better serve students, especially marginalized students.

On the other hand, if you have the sense that your actions aren't aligning with your own internal moral compass this is a sign that you need to do some work reassessing your core values and examining your actions, making any corrections necessary to ensure that your future actions are aligned with your core values. Without self-reflection, unethical practices can become so ingrained and habitual that your brain begins to justify your behavior so that it becomes normalized. This is very dangerous territory. That is why this book advocates continual learning, continual self-reflection, and continual assessment. Using the tools and guidelines provided here will help you avoid the trap of falling into unethical practices and complacency. Principals are very much in the public eye. Unethical or even questionable practices result in principals who are maligned in the news and social media, fired, in legal hot water, or all of the above.

ACTIVITY 3.1

My definition of equity is . . .
I recognize students as individuals when . . .
I initiate courageous conversations when . . .

ACTIVITY 3.2

What Is the One "Sticky" Message You Wish to Share?

What is the one key idea you wish to share with your community right now? You might capture the interest of community members through a carefully crafted story or a thoughtfully devised message. Teachers often hook students through the use of stories; this works just as well with adults as it does with children. People are often able to retell stories better than they can recount facts. It's important to intentionally design a concept that is "sticky." Sticky ideas and messages are simple but memorable because they use vivid words or create an emotional response. Take a few minutes to craft a sticky message that appeals to the heart, fosters connections, or provides direction to your community.

Reflective Questions

- What are some approaches you could use to engage colleagues in conversations about equity and access?
- Identify three actions you might take to support colleagues who are less-equipped to participate in these conversations.
- When might you use data to support an instinct? Which forms of data would you consider?
- Identify a time when you challenged the status quo. What were the circumstances and what was the result? What did you learn from that experience?

PROMOTE AN ETHICAL SCHOOL CULTURE

School leaders are positioned to influence and energize school culture. A significant part of the job involves helping to establish and implement the school's vision and values. The ways in which you represent yourself and publicize your expectations influence people's reactions, which may lead to a highly respected, ethical school culture or could result in a toxic and unethical school culture where staff disregards professional norms and doesn't strive to learn or improve.

Chapter 4 offers suggestions that readers might consider to ensure they "walk the talk." By consistently upholding shared values, the leader develops and maintains an ethical school culture that is positive, inviting, full of life, and learning focused. Those who can successfully and effectively manage school operations while serving as the lead learner in a teaching- and learning-focused community are the leaders who inspire teachers to foster inclusive environments where each individual is welcomed, respected, and motivated to participate in class and school activities. Ethical leaders encourage the people around them to achieve, but without compromising ideals. Hollow victories are unacceptable to upstanding leaders who explicitly model and expect honorable behavior at all levels. As described in Chapter 3, an ethical school culture is characterized by adults who promote democratic values, value diversity, and promote transparency and trust.

STRATEGY #9: WALK THE TALK

The principal is largely the chief architect of the school's climate, culture, and operations. As important as it is for the principal to collaborate with staff to co-create a positive school culture, in the end, the buck stops at the principal's desk. It is the leader whose behavior people watch and take cues from. Leading ethically in diverse communities requires the principal to build capacity in cultural responsiveness while providing spaces for courageous dialogue about instructional practices, curriculum, student learning, and well-being. The school community will pay more attention to what you do than what you say.

BE AN ARCHITECT OF EQUITY

In today's multicultural, pluralistic societies is it possible to be an ethical leader without noticing and addressing the differences that exist between and among students? The National Center for Education Statistics (NCES) reports that the percentage of students in American elementary and secondary public schools who were white decreased from 65% to 49% between 1995 and 2015. During that same period, the percentage of Hispanic students increased from 14% to 26% (NCES, 2018b). Another important concern is the education of refugees from countries throughout the world who have settled in the United States. The Pew Research Center (2018) reports that the largest refugee groups arrived from the Democratic Republic of Congo, Syria, Burma, Iraq, and Somalia. People of Muslim faith made up half of refugee admissions. About 3 million refugees have been resettled in the United States since 1980 (Pew Research Center, 2018).

In addition to increasing racial, ethnic, and religious diversity, there are increasing numbers of students identified with different learning abilities. The percentage of students supported by federal special education programs has risen from 8% to 13% since 1976 (NCES, 2018a). Students with autism make up 1.2% of enrollment in American public schools, while 13% of students have an identified learning disability. A one-size-fits-all approach or curriculum provides limited support to students with an array of needs.

While our communities have become more diverse, the achievement gap between Caucasian students and people of color continues to widen (Genoa, 2016). Ensuring equitable educational opportunities for all children is important to educators, but it is critical to the future of our communities. There are communal benefits that derive from greater educational equity, such as decreases in crimes, lower costs for the penal and judicial systems, more equitable incarceration rates, and "more available male role models in minoritized families" (Shields, 2014, p. 37).

Address Biases in Educational Systems

Ethical educational leadership requires that the principal helps others to identify their own biases, as well as the practices that stigmatize children whose backgrounds differ from the dominant middle-class culture that maintains power. While student populations are increasingly diverse, the teacher and leadership populations remain largely white and middle class; many may not perceive themselves as having a racial identity. Having not prepared for it in their teacher education programs, some may be underprepared to implement culturally responsive teaching and learning strategies (Genoa, 2016) and to be effective teachers across diverse populations. As leaders, we need to fully understand the impact this has on students (Terrell & Lindsey, 2009).

Nelson and Guerra (2014) present information learned following a recent study of educator beliefs and cultural knowledge. The findings from this study demonstrate that a majority of teachers have a general awareness of culture but also have deficit beliefs about diverse students and their families. In describing how they apply cultural knowledge in practice, teachers in this study most frequently named visible aspects of culture and overlooked the less obvious aspects. Little thought was given to the social aspects of education such as language, identity, culture, and relationships, which are the heart of education.

Of important concern is the relationship between an educator's personal beliefs and their professional practice. Our beliefs are powerful filters that shape how we see ourselves, other people, and the world. We hold tightly to these beliefs and rely on them more than knowledge that we acquire from books, courses, and other professional learning opportunities. In other words, "when personal beliefs and professional knowledge conflict, personal beliefs override professional knowledge" (Nelson & Guerra, 2014).

Though educators and students may spend time with each other day after day in the classroom and the school, they may remain strangers to each other. Terrell and Lindsey write, "[the] cultural differences between educator and students are often represented by contrasting experiences, values, beliefs, language, socioeconomics, and worldviews. Educators and students treat one another differently because of a lack of shared experiences" (2009, p. 9). This lack of shared experiences means that teachers continue to teach using traditional methods that worked for them as students; these methods reflect middle-class values that are not optimally effective in promoting the learning of students of color and other groups. Effectively and ethically educating students requires a commitment by teachers and principals to be culturally responsive and sensitive to the particular groups of students in their classrooms and schools. When low performance is evident in a particular minority group, changes may be necessary to the traditional teaching methods to ensure better outcomes. Ethical and equitable leaders can promote innovation in pedagogical practices in order to reverse the effects of low performance by implementing culturally responsive school leadership and culturally responsive student–teacher relationships.

Practice Culturally Responsive School Leadership

To better serve students of color, Muhammad Khalifa (2018) describes three tenets of culturally responsive school leadership:

Tenets of Culturally Responsive School Leadership

1. Cultural responsiveness is a necessary element of school leadership.

2. Cultural responsiveness must be consistently promoted by school leaders.

3. Cultural responsiveness is characterized by a core set of leadership values that include being critically self-reflective, promoting inclusive, anti-oppressive school contexts, and developing and sustaining culturally responsive curricula and teachers.

Some educators suggest fixing achievement gaps by implementing a new program or strategy. Glenn Singleton's work (2018) shows that it is more effective to engage in dialogues to uncover and make sense of the achievement gap at its roots. This means bringing to light the oppressive structures and ways of thinking that led to students' underperformance. Middle-class educators need guidance and opportunities to engage in conversations about race (Singleton, 2018) and activities that foster self-awareness. A *brave space* model, in which conversational norms and boundaries are set, provides a forum for people to discuss beliefs and assumptions about race, gender, class, and other facets of identity. Without these courageous conversations, the achievement gap and the status quo will persist.

Some middle-class educators complain that students who come from impoverished homes are less motivated (the teachers believe) to do well in school. However, the reality is that low performance may be a result of the factors resulting from their home and environment, not of the students' motivation. These students have fewer material goods, limited exposure to language-building opportunities as youngsters, and may receive their most nutritious meals in the school cafeteria. Assumptions that families who live in poverty "care less or have less intrinsic ability to learn is absolutely incorrect and leads to inaction and blaming the victim" (Shields, 2014, p. 34). Courageous conversations should ideally work to bring biases to light so that they can be addressed head-on and so that effective solutions can be formed to close achievement gaps.

Conversations may guide teachers to realize, for example, that young children from inner-cities may have less access to fresh food and may find it more challenging than their affluent peers to recognize, let alone write a multi-paragraph essay about, the various types and properties of fruit. In middle school classrooms, students from impoverished families may struggle with the academic vocabulary and understanding of figurative language needed to make sense of Maya Angelou's poetry. Asking open-ended questions helps educators to assess students' current knowledge and skills so that they can "meet them where they are" and craft instruction to fill gaps in knowledge and provide access to the ways things work in educational systems founded on middle-class values. As a leader, it works best when you recognize the need to meet teachers where they are. Create safe spaces for these courageous conversations to occur. Your staff and teachers need to know and feel that when discussing race, gender, sexual orientation, and other facets of identity, punishment or disdain won't result from them sharing their true feelings or beliefs. Encourage empathy in your teachers by extending your empathy to them.

Students' different backgrounds, cultures, experiences, and values require that we educators develop the ability to be empathic and equity minded. This ability helps us develop equitable processes and curricula that will lead to equitable outcomes for every learner. It is important to remember that whereas "*equal* means everyone gets the same treatment and services as everyone else, *equitable* means each person gets what he or she needs to succeed" (Smith, Frey, Pumpian, & Fisher, 2017, p. 2). Equitable and ethical school leaders are those who do the work to ensure that difficult conversations are happening and that solutions are being crafted, assessed, and revised to ensure that all students are improving academically.

Facilitate Access to the Middle-Class Education System

Leading ethically in diverse communities requires a "two-pronged approach to organizational power" (Shields, 2014, p. 37) that illuminates the realities and rules of educational systems that were founded on middle-class values while helping "outsiders" to gain access to instruction and curriculum. A stance that provides this type of approach is founded on an Ethic of Care, an Ethic of the Profession, and an Ethic of Critique. Ethical leaders ensure that values such as honesty, empathy, responsibility, and excellence are modeled, promoted, and praised. Other values such as racist beliefs and biases must be challenged.

> **Autonomous Systems Leader:** A leader who possess the necessary moral certitude and commitment to disrupt the status quo. Being autonomous implies taking a risk, making a choice, and taking ownership of one's personal actions.

Improving outcomes for all students requires systems leaders who possess moral certitude to upset the apple cart. Disrupting the status quo requires an ability to be an autonomous, independent thinker who will "walk in a direction different from the crowd" if the circumstances are warranted (Starratt, 2014, p. 46). Maintaining existing conditions provides security, and often approval, from those around us. Venturing into the unknown puts us at risk and takes moral courage. Rather than following routine ("that's the way we've always done it"), being autonomous implies choice, responsibility, and ownership of personal actions. In school settings, autonomous thinking is associated with the school staff's willingness to assist minoritized students and families such that they have access to an educational system designed for a different group of people.

Children who come from affluent families are more likely than their lower-income peers to have parents who advocate for them at school and provide them with language and experiences to help them be successful in school. In contrast, children whose parents are not able to help them succeed in the school system—either due to lack of knowledge regarding how the system works, lack of time, or a combination of both— need advocates within the school system to give them an extra helping hand to navigate the sometimes mysterious waters of school system success. Often parents of color and/or economically struggling families don't know what they don't know about the school system—they might not even realize that there are tricks to succeeding. That is where the autonomous systems leaders come in. School employees (principals, teachers, counselors, etc.) understand how the school system works. These individuals can and should take an active interest in identifying students who need this extra help and helping that student by learning more about him or her and providing detailed guidance rather than leaving him to fend for himself. Ethical leaders (and educators) should be courageous enough to notice these discrepancies and take the necessary steps to share access to the system.

There is a timing to disrupting the status quo for long-term change. "Given the multiple rabbit holes of decision making within a school system, a leader must make some strategic choices about how to make change within the local context" (Starr, 2016, p. 73). If you go too fast, you risk offending those who need to "hear" you. If you don't move fast enough, inaction could be harmful to the students and their families who need a champion for their rights. It is helpful to be thoughtful and strategic as to when and how to open these constructive dialogues. The goal is purposeful change that deconstructs previously held assumptions and creates new meaning that is shared by community members.

Strong commitment to providing an equitable education to students doesn't guarantee success on the first try. Don't give up if your motives are called into question. Questioning is part of the process. Mistakes will be made. Allow others, including yourself, to make mistakes without feeling nervous or embarrassed. But to make progress you will need to ask yourself how you will learn from your mistakes. When you as a leader admit that you've made a mistake and then discuss aloud the thinking that led to your error, you model a process that prioritizes honesty and relationships over being perfect. People will lean in to listen when a leader admits to a mistake and then shares how a different course of action would have been a better choice. Be genuine during these conversations because people recognize a phony.

MODEL INNOVATION AND EMPATHY

Leaders can teach by example by sharing their own learning experiences with others. Articulating a snapshot of the methodical thinking that led to a particular result allows others to visualize themselves in that situation. "Mentorship, inquiry into complex problems, and dialogue" (Goodwin, 2017) help people build their own critical thinking skills and empathy and gives others a model to draw from when they face similar challenges.

A learning culture is one that promotes emotional safety, so publicize expectations for stepping up when mistakes are made. "People want to know and trust their leaders, rather than be dazzled by their charisma" (Branson, 2014, p. 439). When people feel safe and consider the leader to be an ethical person, they are more likely to come forward and admit the mistake. On the flip side, when leaders rule with an iron fist and condemn mistakes, people may lie to cover up their errors. Without emotional safety and an understanding of a growth mindset, coverups may result. What was initially an honest mistake may escalate to an ethical violation if a transgression is hushed up. Telling the truth saves time, energy, and reputations. There will be a healthier culture when everyone works together to fix problems instead of hiding them.

Educators often need to think out the box to come up with effective solutions for persistent problems rather than relying on canned solutions from the past. But this won't happen if people don't think they have permission to experiment with innovative solutions. Leaders who promote thoughtful risk-taking in a safe environment cultivate a culture of people who weigh the odds before making big decisions. In contrast, leaders who punish experiments gone badly stifle innovation and creativity, therefore promoting the status quo. Empowering your staff to try things and expressing empathy when mistakes are made demonstrates trust in their decision-making processes. People appreciate having their judgment valued by their boss.

PROVIDE CLEAR RATIONALE FOR DECISIONS

Starr (2016) asserts that decision making is one of the least understood aspects of school systems. Who decides what curriculum is purchased and how frequently students are tested? How are students assigned to classes? Who sets policies, and which ones are strictly enforced? If the nitty-gritty of school governance is rarely discussed, the school community may have a limited or partial understanding of what goes on behind the scenes. In the absence of information, people often develop their own theories that may or may not be true.

Integrity, transparency, and communication are hallmarks of effective and ethical governance. While people might comment about your leadership style, never let them say you don't have integrity. "People will inevitably disagree with a leader's decision at some point, but if the decision-making process has integrity, the leader may get benefit of the doubt that it was necessary" (Starr, 2016). What might seem obvious to you may not be obvious to others. When appropriate, communicate the rationale and intentions behind the decisions you make.

It is important to articulate your thinking processes aloud, as this practice not only cements your reputation as a systematic thinker but also invites others to weigh in with their own opinions. When people know the goals you are trying to achieve, they will be able to offer more insightful and helpful suggestions that you might not have considered. Regularly seeking feedback helps you to assess the quality of your decisions while being transparent to the community. Research from Nei and Nei (2018) suggests that new leaders tend to be mindful of initial impressions but may spend less time interacting with others as they become more comfortable in their positions. Regularly reminding yourself to check in with others and solicit feedback about ongoing initiatives will keep your thinking fresh and focused on the ultimate goal.

Managing Yourself Isn't Enough

While publicizing your own high standards is a good start, it's not enough to sustain an ethical school culture. You must also be vigilant of others' standards and behaviors. Are there any questionable practices occurring in classrooms or on the playground? Have you noticed instances when no one speaks up? A responsibility of an ethical leader is to listen to what people say, and what they don't say. Holte (2009) asserts that there is a "hidden curriculum of silence in schools." She refers to this phenomenon as the "curriculum silentium" and explains that it influences the ethical judgments made by school staff members to the point of encouraging them to turn a blind eye and remain silent when observing unethical actions. In this type of culture, school employees perceive that speaking up is too risky for them.

When a culture of silence manifests in a school, the results can be devastating. A study by Aronsson and Gustafsson (1999, as cited by Holte, 2014) reported that 40% of teachers felt they were met with resistance from the school leader when they tried to speak up about ethical issues. Following this type of encounter, the teacher may be ignored or experience negative sanctions. When a teacher feels silenced, he or she is unlikely to engage in constructive dialogue because of fear. Another affect that may occur is the teacher rationalizes why silence is the best option. It appears that silence, rather than speaking up, about unethical practices is more common than one may realize (Holte, 2014).

Perhaps there are some people on your campus who could benefit from explicit guidance on ethical and equitable practices. Make it known that you will not tolerate unethical behaviors, and nor should they. If you ignore a staff member's silence, lackluster attitude, or near-sighted views, there is a risk of offending others and disgracing your organization. An ethical culture is promoted by the sharing of values and viewpoints such that meaning can be jointly negotiated and all parties can understand each other. "In times of unpredictability and insecurity, people want their leaders to bring some form of certainty and order to their worlds" (Branson, 2014, p. 451). Spaces for thoughtful and open communication provides a forum for people to understand your motives and take cues from you. When a lapse in judgment occurs, it is an opportunity for you to engage in a private conversation with an individual. These types of conversations, which are often difficult, establish your ethical mindset and provide an opportunity for the colleague to continue to grow. In addition to informal conversations about the issue, formal communications should be also be scheduled to ensure reflection has occurred and to deepen the relationship with that person.

Honor the Achievements and Struggles of Your Staff

Responding with empathy when teachers make mistakes is important. It is just as important to celebrate and praise teachers when they have achieved a particularly difficult goal or have pulled off an innovative lesson. Part of building an ethical and positive school culture means providing honest and differentiated feedback for every member of the school community. Have you ever been a part of an organization that didn't acknowledge you positively or negatively? How did that feel? People need, and deserve, feedback that tells them they are doing well or acknowledges their struggle and offers them encouragement and constructive advice on how to improve. When it is obvious that someone is having difficulty, good leaders ask the right questions and provide appropriate support. When someone is doing really well or has overcome a particularly difficult milestone, it is important to honor that achievement and acknowledge it personally and publicly.

Unfortunately, there may be times when a teacher is just not the right fit for your school. While we want to see each person bloom where they are planted, sometimes people need a change of scenery in order to bloom. Feedback may help them to refocus and find a more suitable workplace. As much as we would like every person to share our beliefs and be a part of "our team," that's not a realistic belief. Allow people the space to grow in different directions. Grant them permission to join another team. Permitting those individuals to explore more suitable working environments will ultimately elevate staff and school morale because you can reallocate your energy to those who believe in your school's vision and values.

CHARACTERISTICS OF CONSTRUCTIVE DIALOGUE

Constructive dialogue is a type of communication that encourages thinking and creativity while providing coherence to sometimes undeveloped or unrelated ideas. It allows points of uneasiness to surface and then resolves them by exposing pertinent perspectives. Constructive dialogue is a process of intellectual inquiry; instead of advocating for a particular outcome, an exploration for truth drives the discussion. People are more likely to feel emotionally committed to the eventual outcome.

When teachers are empowered to help shape an outcome, they are more likely to feel energized and involved in the effort (Sacks, 2017). It is critical that the leader is deliberate in creating the space for teachers and staff members to engage in constructive dialogue, as this type of communication is best facilitated by protocols that ensure voices are heard and that time is used efficiently. Constructive dialogue occurs in cultures that are dedicated to being productive and decision driven. It is wise to be mindful of the social structures inherent in groups. Tool 4.1 offers strategies to overcome dynamics that may undermine group processing.

TOOL 4.1

Strategies for Responding to Dialogue Pitfalls

Constructive Dialogue Killer	Solution
Self-interests undermine group interests	Ensure the meeting purpose supports actions and services for students.
Aimless meetings where nothing gets done	Use established protocols and communicate success criteria for every meeting.
Necessary information is not shared	Build trust and ensure each person feels safe and has space to share relevant material.
There is no "next step" at the end of the meeting	Co-develop next steps with the group and establish a timeline for implementation.

Too often the focus on ethical leadership is confined only to school leaders (Tuana, 2014). However, in order to truly have a healthy school climate, teachers also need opportunities to learn and model ethical practices with each other as well as with students. Constructive dialogue provides a forum for learning about real problems. It is typically used to solve problems where a technical solution doesn't exist. For example, a problem related to student achievement or student well-being surfaces and people are motivated to identify potential contributing causes and generate possible solutions. This type of dialogue is characterized by four features: openness, candor, informality, and closure (Charan, 2006).

Openness

Be open to ideas that differ from your own. Do not begin a meeting with a predetermined outcome. Encourage a genuine exploration of different perspectives and new ideas. The principal's willingness to hear others' viewpoints is illuminated by questions such as, "What don't we know?" and "What are your thoughts about . . . ?" When the principal creates a safe environment that promotes trust, intellectual engagement, and collective learning, people will lean in. It's not just the principal who needs to be open, but the principal is responsible for modeling behavior, setting norms, and holding people accountable for following those norms during meetings.

Being open means that people feel empowered to jointly determine decisions around instructional programs, strategies, and use of data to inform next steps for individual students and programs. This means that people are open to a discussion of current realities and ideas for improvement. An example could be a discussion involving a recent analysis of formative data showing that one group of students didn't make enough progress in math. A structured discussion about the students' errors, instructional techniques to address those errors, and timeframe for intervention to occur is necessary. Professional Standards for Educational Leaders professional norms place students at the center of education and remind us that we are responsible for each student's academic success and well-being. When we engage in open discussions about our current teaching practices, we are more likely to identify alternative strategies that assist students in their learning. Being open means that we are willing to adjust practices to better meet the needs of individual students.

Candor

Candor is the ability to say what has been unspoken, to nudge people to be deeply genuine, and to shed light on any disagreements that may compromise consensus. People are candid when they express their honest opinions, not what they think others would like them to say. Since trust is a precursor to candor, leaders must ensure that people see it and feel it. It is only when there is a trusting environment that people who were partially committed will have the courage to be honest. When the environment and climate is such that candor is promoted, the resulting open dialogue will ensure that there will be less resistance to solution implementation. If people silently disagree with the group decision, they likely have no intention to assist in the implementation effort. By encouraging people to be candid, there will be less need to revisit decisions that were not owned by all members of the group.

In school settings, moral courage is needed for candor to illuminate issues that affect individual students and groups of students. Being candid enables groups to question community-shared prejudices, such as racism or sexism, that have been normalized in the school. These types of dialogues deepen commitment to shared values and helps to minimize ethical insensitivity by exposing blind spots that impede student learning and well-being.

Informality

While protocols are useful for efficiency, dialogue may be more productive when the tone doesn't feel too formal. Authenticity is boosted when people feel free to express viewpoints and learn in the moment. Scripted presentations and discussions usually indicate that the meeting outcomes were preplanned and the meeting was simply a formality. People may feel disengaged when it's obvious that their input will bear no weight on the impending decision. In contrast, questions that ask for a free response from participants imply that conversations are open-ended and there is a genuine interest in generating thought-provoking discussion that furthers the group's understanding of an issue. In an open climate, people feel more comfortable asking questions because they know that their input is directing the course of the conversation. We act more honestly and sincerely when we know that we are helping to shape the outcome of a decision.

For example, during a discussion about immigrant students' language acquisition, it's important that people participate with an open mind. Instead of relying upon past practices, consider what is known about this student, or this family, and how might the school respond to their specific needs. It is through these authentic discussions that school systems become more responsive and create equitable conditions (McNae, 2014, p. 97).

Closure

Finally, once good dialogue has occurred, the strategic influencer ensures time for closure before the group moves to another item or adjourns. Providing time for closure while everyone is still in the room ensures clarity and accountability—people should understand what they are supposed to do and when they are supposed to do it. Without closure, we run the risk of people leaving the room with questions in their minds.

To ensure that student well-being and learning is at the center of all decision making on campus, it is important to have protocols in place that ensure clarity and accountability among all staff. Since teachers and staff members make hundreds of choices each day, it's imperative that the teachers—not just the school leader—model and promote principles of equity and inclusivity at all times. School leaders must rely on staff to actualize inclusive conditions throughout all areas of the physical structure of the school itself, as well as school-related functions.

THE CASE OF RELATIONSHIP BUILDING
LEADING TO STUDENT SUCCESS

Principal Perry
Elementary School
Washington State

A principal we'll call Mr. Perry was assigned to a low-performing school we'll call Evergreen Elementary following the previous administrator's departure under questionable circumstances. The former principal had quit before the last school year had ended, leaving the community without a leader for the final month of school. No one knew why she had left but speculated that it was because student achievement was low. As a result, teachers and staff felt abandoned and the school culture was suffering. Principal Perry, a go-getter, was charged with raising student achievement.

While Principal Perry had a firm grasp on effective instruction, he slowed his usual tempo and began to ask questions of the teachers and staff. He appeared to not be in a hurry to make any quick changes. Instead, Principal Perry focused on talking to as many students and adults as he could. He approached conversations and meetings openly, inquiring about lessons, strategies, and school culture from a place of honesty and sincerity. Through these interactions, Principal Perry developed relationships, heard their concerns, and demonstrated an authentic leadership style that conveyed warmth and humor.

These conversations led to a deeper understanding of the school and its needs, and they also earned Principal Perry the respect and trust of the staff and community. Instead of telling teachers what the achievement data said, he asked for their input to make sense of the numbers. When it was time to plan instructional improvements, Principal Perry assembled a team to help shape professional development. Principal Perry understood that people value relationships over initiatives. He knew that instructional improvement would not occur if it were demanded of teachers. Instead, Principal Perry used his people skills to unite groups of people around core values and a shared purpose.

Principal Perry began the school improvement effort by focusing on culture. Deliberate moves to elevate culture led to early wins; staff and students quickly began to feel a more upbeat tone. Principal Perry made it a point to learn every student's name. He tried to greet students every morning as they arrived to school. Other simple ideas such as having a "Joke of the Week" with students led to amusement and language development. Principal Perry poured root beer floats for staff on a Friday afternoon so they could "float away." These gestures, while small, began to add up and first-semester formative data indicated that students were learning at greater rates than previous years.

The success that everyone felt at Evergreen Elementary was facilitated by Principal Perry. He didn't demand change or berate staff for poor performance. Instead, he demonstrated collaborative leadership by assembling leadership teams that had a true voice in the development of a shared vision. He provided guidance and time frames, fostering a sense of commitment toward increased student outcomes as well as a healthy school culture.

Starratt (2014) reminds us that "cultivating an ethical school, then, calls for great courage; a modicum of intelligence, lots of humility, and an unyielding hope in the potential, endurance, and heroism of human beings" (p. 60). Ethical and positive school culture needs constant nourishment that is fueled by openness, candor, and informality that leads to clarity and accountability for student well-being and academic success. It works best when the leader doesn't talk down to people, but continually strives to articulate his or her thinking such that community members understand clear rationale for decisions and also have opportunities to voice their opinions without fear of punishment or embarrassment. An ethical and positive school culture provides opportunities for the school leader to become a strategic influencer.

STRATEGY #10: BECOME A STRATEGIC INFLUENCER

The final strategy offered in this book is to learn how to strategically influence change instead of demanding it. Ethical school leadership is multidimensional; an unwavering commitment to one's ideals is a first step, but achieving outcomes of inclusion and equity takes collaboration, coordination, and leading with moral courage. Since leaders are continually in the spotlight, we must be prepared for the complex and unique challenges that arise. Often a challenge becomes a defining moment for the leader.

DEFINING MOMENTS

Throughout this book, dilemmas have been presented as a means to learn from the actions of others. The cases presented here were defining moments for the principals in those stories. Have you experienced a defining moment when your professional obligations unexpectedly clashed with your core values? Examples might include declining enrollment forces a principal to release his best teacher; your daughter's prom is on the same night as your school's graduation ceremony; or your actions toward inclusion are negatively portrayed by social media. During these conflicts, we struggle with right vs. right choices. Regardless of which "right" we choose, we almost always feel like we're wronging someone. These decisions ultimately cement the foundation of our character. For this reason, they are called *defining moments*.

What is the difference between a tough choice and a defining moment? A tough choice usually involves choosing between two options: one option that we believe to be right and the other we believe to be wrong. A defining moment, however, challenges us in a more profound way by forcing us to choose between two or more of our own values. These types of situations rarely offer an easy or correct response. Instead, these situations compel us to dig deep into our souls. When we finally commit to a permanent course of action after considerable deliberation, we take another step toward defining our character, both personally and professionally.

Since leaders are charged with developing and reaching achievement and climate goals with our school community, it is important to note that ethical leaders do not make demands of their constituents. Rather, ethical leaders are skilled in facilitation and negotiation; these are skills necessary for building consensus and influencing change. The leader, when acting as a strategic influencer, identifies and removes obstacles that stand in the way of reaching a goal. A strategic influencer also initiates conversations that need to occur with individuals and groups such that learning takes place and growth toward a goal occurs. Long-range planning is a strength of a strategic influencer and he or she uses his or her understanding of human capital to mobilize people toward that shared vision. Taking strategic steps, underpinned by an understanding of motivational techniques, will assist you to become a strategic influencer on your campus.

Defining Moments Are Public

When we act during a defining moment, we announce an aspect of our character to those around us. Defining moments expose a piece of us that was previously hidden. It is during these moments that our strength of character is tested; we learn if we are able to stay true to our own ideals. Part of being a public persona is making a conscious effort to communicate who you are and what you stand for to those you serve.

One way to ensure consistent messaging is by establishing routines and mechanisms for communication that others can come to expect. E-mail, staff meetings, newsletters, and social media can all be leveraged to craft the story of your leadership and the story of your school (Sheninger, 2014). Remember that others may also use these tools (particularly social media) to garner support to oppose your decisions, muddy your character, or to be the first one to break the story.

It is important to establish a reputation for yourself that transcends any commentary that may be published on social media. You can cement a reputation as an ethical, trustworthy, and caring leader who prioritizes students' well-being and community interests over self-interests. When difficult situations arise, it is helpful if your school community knows that you walk the talk and that your actions are pure. Your consistent attention to ethical leadership paints a picture of how you will handle any situation that arises. Community members, staff and parents alike, are more apt to support you during defining moments if you've proven to be a fair and ethical leader.

Comprehensive Communication

An aspect of being a strategic influencer is the ability to adjust communication to people based upon their preferred modalities and personality. For instance, there are those who receive feedback that is given in person, such as two-way conversations that occur where meaning is jointly negotiated. Others prefer written communication so that they have the opportunity to think before responding. A strategic influencer proactively learns each person's preferences and plans interactions that capitalize on each person's communication styles. This knowledge fosters deeper connections with each person such that the key messages are more likely to stick. You will find additional strategies for listening generously in Chapter 2.

In addition to adjusting communication modalities, strategic influencers also use all tools at their disposal to best communicate messages to the community. Tools include social media, memos, blogs, and digital text and voice communications that can be sent to community members. Horizontal communication helps teachers to respond well to challenges and strengthens teachers' professional development (Sacks,

2017). Skilled principals look at every social interaction as an opportunity to further a message, praise positive behavior and accomplishments, and deepen commitment to shared values.

Are You Ready for Your Next Defining Moment?

When we are asked to identify important meetings that are coming up, we have to glance at a calendar, but it's not usually a difficult task. What is more challenging is pinpointing two or three moments in an upcoming meeting that will define its outcomes. Often we don't have a problem with discerning the critical moments from our past, but predicting and preparing for those critical moments in the future is usually more difficult. Hsieh (2010) calls these instances "moments of truth" because the outcome is hanging in the balance and is being decided in real time. During a moment of truth, the outcome could go either way—positively or negatively.

It is during these moments of truth that preparation and well-considered strategy come into play. While it's not possible to prepare for every event that could happen, strategic influencers consider multiple angles and solutions before problems arise. Instead of being caught off-guard or feeling paralyzed by circumstances, strategic influencers are prepared to suggest solutions that match the vision and values of the school community. Being open to new ideas is part of being prepared—you have already envisioned the situation from multiple angles and are able to offer solutions that are a win–win for everybody.

The ability to find a win–win for everybody results from the knowledge that uncertainty occurs at least once during most important meetings. This means that before every important meeting, you might consider thinking about what the moments might be. It might be useful to visualize the interactions and determine where you might make some strategic suggestions. It's not possible to know all of the "moves" ahead of time, so your preparation allows you to be mentally alert and ready to respond when opportunities emerge. Those who take advantage of these moments of truth are likely those who will influence the outcome. Being mentally prepared and upholding your core values will help to ensure a moment of truth becomes a breakthrough moment.

Ethical leaders see the big picture because they are able to reflect back while steering the group forward. Knowledge of past problems helps the leader to pinpoint a problem and address it before it explodes into a crisis. The same is true for defining moments when working with groups of people. These moments should be viewed as a part of a bigger process that needs to be understood and managed. A Chinese proverb that is relevant here: "The best time to plant a tree was 20 years ago. The second-best time is now." Keeping this principle in mind, it behooves leaders to think ahead and identify desirable outcomes. Successful leaders establish the conditions for an effective, and ethical, resolution to a defining moment well in advance of when a situation pops up. Principal Walker (a pseudonym) in the case that follows did just that by setting an example that his staff (unbeknownst to him) began to emulate.

THE CASE OF THE NEW COMMUNITY MEMBER

Principal Walker
Middle School
Tennessee

Principal Walker was the principal of Southeast Middle School in a suburban area that traditionally served white students from middle-class homes. Demographics of the school began to change as waves of immigrants from Eritrea, Somalia, the Middle East, and Central America arrived and resettled in the area. The changing demographics were immediately noticed by the staff, but they nonetheless continued their usual teaching practices.

Soon it was apparent that many of the newcomers were struggling to understand academic concepts, and some families appeared uninterested in school functions or attending parent conferences. A divide between the kids whose family members had attended the school for generations and the newcomers was evident: the divide between the "haves" and "have nots" was clearly visible, and the staff was unprepared for these changes. They perceived the new families to be apathetic and uninterested in learning English and American ways.

Principal Walker had a system of collecting formative assessment data from teachers every quarter. He had established a process for progress monitoring with teachers, and this information was shared with parents in quarterly progress reports. Parents were mailed the progress reports and students were required to return a signed copy to their homeroom teachers. For years, this system had worked, in that teachers submitted grades, students returned the documents, and teachers worked with parents to shore up areas of need. The system started to break down when many of the new students didn't return their signed progress reports. When teachers reminded students of this requirement, students said they would try to bring them but few did.

Principal Walker and the staff were perplexed. They had been successful a short time ago and now felt unequipped to meet the needs of their new students; further, they really didn't want to change their ways. To complicate matters, there was a lack of adults to serve as translators between their native language and English to facilitate communication between the home and the school. Student achievement was suffering, and Principal Walker was concerned that while his staff was well intentioned, they weren't reaching the immigrant students.

Intent on providing assistance to help the newcomers, Principal Walker repeatedly asked his district for additional resources but none were available. He began to research the newcomers' countries of origin to learn their customs and values. Eid, an Islamic holiday that Principal Walker was unfamiliar with, was approaching and he wondered if stronger ties between the school and the community could be established if the school acknowledged the holiday. When he began to ask students and families, Principal Walker was surprised by how quickly community members and students wanted to talk about their traditions and the meanings behind them. Principal Walker had numerous conversations with community members and encouraged staff to show an interest in their students' home cultures.

Not all staff was as open as Principal Walker, and it took some persuasion to convince teachers to provide small-group instruction to meet the needs of all learners, but many were coming around and began to view other cultures with open minds. A pivotal moment occurred when a parent of Islamic faith, who we'll call Mr. Hussein, volunteered to talk to all students during a Career Day assembly about his work in the technology industry. Career Week had been a tradition at Southeast Middle; parents and other community members were invited to give 20-minute talks about their professions during scheduled morning assemblies over a week-long period.

Principal Walker felt that some staff members might have doubts about Mr. Hussein's presentation. He felt they might worry that Mr. Hussein might say something controversial because of his faith, students might misconstrue his message, or the minority students might be teased because of his appearance. Principal Walker assured them that he would personally monitor the parents' sentiments and promote multiculturalism with students. He viewed it as a learning opportunity for students and staff and would send a message to the community that the school valued diversity.

On the morning when Mr. Hussein was scheduled to speak, Principal Walker was woken by his wife who was experiencing terrible abdominal pains. Ms. Walker was clearly in agony and needed urgent medical attention. It was determined that her appendix burst and she needed immediate surgery. Principal Walker felt conflicted: he had to be there for his wife's surgery, but he wanted to be on hand for the assembly to ensure it went well. This was a defining moment for Principal Walker. While his commitment to the school was strong, his loyalty to his wife was greater and her health was his top priority.

Principal Walker called his secretary from the hospital and explained the situation. He asked that she cancel the assembly and call Mr. Hussein and apologize on his behalf. His secretary suggested that the assembly go on as planned, that she would apprise the lead teachers of Mrs. Walker's condition, and ask if they could step in to open the assembly and introduce Mr. Hussein. His secretary had observed the changing demographics and was empathetic to new families as they enrolled their children in the school. She felt that canceling the assembly would send the wrong message to the community. Principal Walker agreed, but nonetheless he worried about the whole situation as well as his wife's health.

What Principal Walker didn't know is that his inclusive leadership was observed and appreciated by more staff members than he realized. Many staff members stepped up and led discussions with students before and after the assembly, ensuring Mr. Hussein's message was received positively and students were given insight into another culture and career path. Mrs. Walker recovered from appendicitis and when Principal Walker returned to Southeast Middle, he was engaged in numerous conversations with students, staff, and the community about the week's assemblies. He was very pleased to learn that Mr. Hussein, as well as the other Career Day speakers, had made positive impressions on the students; a few conveyed that they were inspired to follow their dreams and were willing to tackle challenges along the way.

MENTAL PREPARATION

Mental preparation means that you reflect back on previous events but also look forward to an ideal state of the school. This means that while past actions have some bearing, we should learn from mistakes and keep others' positions in mind. Strategic influencers don't leave outcomes to chance. They comprehend the skills, knowledge, dispositions, and values that will guide the school community to the next level and have intentionally prepared by visualizing future conversations with individuals and groups.

To take your school to the next level, it is recommended that you take time to clearly understand the vision, define long-term goals, and determine intermediate steps. Achieving long-term goals can't be done by making demands, so consider how you might foster conditions that people begin to take steps toward the vision on their own. The idea is to get people to see and be genuinely committed to taking steps toward the vision by using your professional influence. Leaving outcomes to chance will not help to eliminate the achievement gap or make kids feel valued at school. A useful analogy here is the idea of dropping "bread crumbs" during conversations that spark others' thinking. These bread crumbs are invitations for people to think differently and be motivated to engage in conversations and dialogues when you're not there. Essentially, you are empowering people to be intentional about teaching and learning practices that foster greater equity and access. The best initiatives are those that form organically from the ground up.

FACILITATE WIN–WIN SITUATIONS

Your ability to see the big picture and build partnerships leads to a deeper shared purpose and the creation of coalitions. When people feel included to help shape the direction of the school, they breathe life into programs and initiatives and become co-producers of a movement toward the next level. It is more productive and a greater sense of commitment is developed when people are energized around a common mission. Strategic influencers do not demand change but strategically influence people using skills of planning ahead, questioning, facilitation, and negotiation.

Some questions to consider to facilitate win–win situations

- Have I ensured that discussions and conversations are inclusive?
- How can I ensure that conflicts are effectively resolved?
- How do I ensure that people arrive at a consensus and feel dialogues are win–win?

Skills of negotiation and facilitation here are described in the context of teaching and learning. It's important that the groups are focused on what matters most: student learning. We keep this goal at the forefront by focusing discussions on instruction and culture. For example, attendance rate data analysis may reveal that a group of students, such as students with disabilities, is absent more frequently than other groups. Instead of using deficit language, such as "those kids can't learn if they're not in school," work with your groups to determine contributing factors for why the kids aren't in school and focus on what is within your control. Is it a matter of illness? Do students feel welcomed when they are at school? What can we do to make school a more attractive place where students want to be in class? Perhaps low attendance rates are a result of practices at the school level that need to be examined and improved.

Data analysis in school settings is far greater than identifying achievement gaps. The strategic influencer is adept in leading these processes but also is conscious of leading with core values and guiding people to identify new ways for students to grasp material instead of blaming them for not learning. This means that one-size-fits-all remedies rarely work for students, especially students of color, so it's important that the principal models a growth mindset that is inquiry-based.

Systemic transformation for equity should not be a compliance-oriented exercise. It works best when grounded in intentional efforts that develop and sustain a school culture in which all students, staff, and families learn and grow through their most empowered selves. Building the capacity to effectively deliver a high-quality education to every child is the "right thing to do morally and the smart thing to do economically" (Childress, 2009, p. 18).

NEVER STOP LEARNING AND GROWING

Problematic situations will always arise, but making ethical and equitable decisions becomes easier when you collaborate with the school community and use shared values to guide your way. Being an ethical leader takes moral courage. Courageous leadership counteracts prejudices by opening spaces and dialogues for students and community members to grow. Continual investments in the professional learning and school culture reap many rewards, including more inclusive classrooms where students feel valued, respected, and challenged to excel.

Being an ethical person is not a "one and done." Learning the difference between right and wrong as a child is a first step, but it isn't enough. Continual reflection and a desire to continue to learn and grow is necessary to maintain moral fitness, especially in today's diverse schools. When leaders are able to create the conditions for community members to be open and reflective, students also benefit because they internalize tenets of ethical behavior. Ethical behavior is a lifelong pursuit.

Ethical school leaders are transparent and purposefully create cultures that are inclusive to all students. These leaders are strategic influencers and walk the talk. They effectively respond to the problems that naturally arise, but they also strive to prevent discrimination and prejudice. Our students need leaders who provide increased access to the education system so that they are academically successful and well-prepared to be productive community members and leaders. As the school leader, it may seem like a "big ask" but it's your professional responsibility and obligation to the students in your charge. Consider how you might create the conditions for equitable education in Activity 4.1.

ACTIVITY 4.1

I will commit to improving access to the education system by . . .
You will be able to see multicultural values at my school when . . .
My commitment to mentorship is seen when . . .
My responsibility to my school community is . . .

Reflective Questions

Questions to Consider for Promoting an Ethical School Culture

- Am I leading with my core values?
- How can I foster a school climate where staff and parents use asset-based language to engage in data analysis and determine next steps?
- How do I ensure that staff and community members work together to identify root causes when students underperform?
- Am I demonstrating passion and enthusiasm by modeling asset-based language that doesn't blame the victims?
- How do I facilitate conversations that inspire people to reject outdated programs and design learning experiences that meet students where they are?
- What are my next steps?
- How will I contribute to making my school a community center?
- How will I nurture my school culture so that it is ethical and equitable?

CONCLUSION

Successful and effective leadership in today's diverse school communities is challenging work. Professional judgment about educational ethics requires the insights of thoughtful practitioners who use their repertoire of instructional, organizational, pedagogical, and cultural leadership to make sense of problems and a wide range of actions. Nonpractitioners may only see a binary decision between two decisions: suspend a student or make it a teachable moment? Educators who remain true to their Ethical Line often see novel options to thorny challenges and understand that every ethical dilemma presents a complex web of personalities, cultures, practices, politics, rules, and legal requirements that must be explored and resolved. While theories are certainly useful in the development of one's vision and philosophy, it is a particular skill set, coupled with emotional intelligence, that is needed to cut through racialized patterns of discipline or refine instructional strategies to be more culturally responsive.

With so many compelling and competing issues at stake, what does responsible decision making look like? I believe that it requires looking for solutions that meet multiple priorities simultaneously, with the ultimate goal of finding balance between different goods. It is a conscious effort to further what is good for the individual, what is good for the organization, and what is good for the community.

It is as important that we develop as ethical decision makers as it is important to develop ethical school systems. That's the work of today's school principal. We must continually self-reflect but also challenge ourselves and others to think about problems from systemic levels as well. Building better systems means that school leaders make decisions for students based upon how the system should ideally work, instead of relying on traditional assumptions about how the system currently functions. Without courageous leadership, oppressive systems endure and fail many students.

Staying true to your Ethical Line and adhering to what is in the best interests of all students demonstrates a higher standard of ethical behavior on your school campus. Don't allow the demands of others or past practices to distort your thinking when you engage in a complex challenge. Don't be dissuaded by limited resources, naysayers, or other constraints. With patience, insight, and flexible thinking, you will come to a well-reasoned and feasible conclusion about how to navigate the challenge.

As public school leaders, we have a responsibility to secure a minimum level of educational opportunities for *every* student in our charge. Since students come to us with differing levels of advantage, we must prioritize the needs of our most disadvantaged students and provide the necessary interventions or differentiated support so that they are prepared to meet educational benchmarks that prepare them to be critical thinkers who are well-adjusted to actively participate in a democratic society. When these outcomes are realized, our work as ethical leaders is realized.

IMPLEMENTATION STEPS

Now that you have reached this point, what actions will you commit to when you face a dilemma at your school?

Reflective Questions

- What steps will you take to frame the issue?
- How will your core values intersect with your approach to an issue?
- Which colleagues will you approach for advice and counsel? Identify three or four people now.
- Whose interests should be given priority? Why?
- What are you trying to accomplish in the short term? What are possible long-term consequences of your actions?

REFERENCES

Achor, S., & Gielan, M. (2016). Resilience is about how you recharge, not how you endure. *Harvard Business Review.*

Alvoid, L., & Black, W. L. (2014). The changing role of the principal. Center for American Progress. Retrieved from https://www.americanprogress.org/issues/education-k-12/reports/2014/07/01/93015/the-changing-role-of-the-principal/

Branch, G. F., Hanushek, E. A., & Rivkin, S. G. (2013). Estimating the effect of leaders on public sector productivity: The case of school principals. *Center for Analysis of Longitudinal Data in Education Research, January 2012.* Retrieved from http://www.caldercenter.org/sites/default/files/Hanushek_wp66.pdf

Branson, C. M. (2014). Maintaining moral integrity. In C. M. Branson & S. J. Gross (Eds.), *Handbook of ethical educational leadership.* New York: Routledge.

Branston, J. (2013). The curious case of Clarence Mumford. *Memphis Flyer.* https://www.memphisflyer.com/CityBeatBlog/archives/2013/02/01/the-curious-case-of-clarence-mumford

Bush, B. (2017). Five years in, cases linger in Columbus schools data cheating scandal. *The Columbus Dispatch.* Retrieved from https://www.dispatch.com/news/20170616/five-years-in-cases-linger-in-columbus-schools-data-cheating-scandal

Carter, C. J. (2013). Grand jury indicts 35 in Georgia school cheating scandal. *CNN.* https://www.cnn.com/2013/03/29/us/georgia-cheating-scandal/index.html

Charan, R. (2006). Conquering a culture of indecision. *Harvard Business Review.*

Childress, S. M. (2009). Six lessons for pursuing excellence and equity at scale. *Kappan, 91,* 3.

Chussil, M. (2016). Keep a list of unethical things you'll never do. *Harvard Business Review.*

Cranston, N., Ehrich, L. C., & Kimber, M. (2014). Managing ethical dilemmas. In C. M. Branson & S. J. Gross (Eds.), *Handbook of ethical educational leadership.* New York: Routledge.

Cuddy, A. J. C. (2015). *Presence: Bringing your boldest self to your biggest challenges.* New York: Little, Brown and Company.

Daimler, M. (2016). Listening is an overlooked leadership tool. *Harvard Business Review.*

Darden, E. C. (2014). Ethics at school: Let your conscience be your guide. *Kappan, 95*(5), 70–71.

Davis, S. H. (2005). What was I thinking? *School Administrator, 96*(6), 36–41.

DeWitt, P. M. (2017). *Collaborative leadership.* Thousand Oaks, CA: Corwin.

Dipping, C. (2012). 12-ton dirt pile removed from Southwest High football field. *The San Diego Union-Tribune.* Retrieved from https://www.sandi egouniontribune.com/sdut-12-ton-dirt-pile-removed-southwest-high-football-f-2012aug17-story.html

Donohoo, J. (2017). *Collective efficacy.* Thousand Oaks, CA: Corwin.

Emmons, R. A., & McCullough, M. (2003). Counting blessings versus burdens: An experimental investigation of gratitude and subjective well-being in daily life. *Journal of Personality and Social Psychology, 84*(2), 377–389.

Ethics and Compliance Initiative. (2019a). Ethics filters. https://www.ethics .org/resources/free-toolkit/decision-making-model/#filters

Ethics and Compliance Initiative. (2019b). The PLUS Ethical Decision Making Model. https://www.ethics.org/resources/free-toolkit/decision-making-model/

Eyal, O., Berkovich, I., & Schwartz, T. (2010). Making the right choices: Ethical judgments among educational leaders. *Journal of Educational Administration, 49*(4), 396–413.

Franz, A. (2013). Prison time for some Atlanta school educators in cheating scandal. *CNN.* https://www.cnn.com/2015/04/14/us/georgia-atlanta-pub lic-schools-cheating-scandal-verdicts/index.html

Frick, W. C., Bass, L., & Young, M. D. (2018). Preface. In *Developing ethical principles for school leadership.* New York: Routledge.

Gallagher, A., & Thordarson, K. (2018). *Design thinking for school leaders.* Alexandria, VA: ASCD.

Genoa, S. (2016). Culturally responsive pedagogy: Reflections on mentoring by educational leadership candidates. *Issues in Educational Research, 26*(3), 431–445.

Gino, F., & Grant, A. (2013). The big benefits of a little thanks. *Harvard Business Review.* https://hbr.org/2013/11/the-big-benefits-of-a-little-thanks

Goleman, D. (2004). The five components of emotional intelligence at work. *Harvard Business Review.*

Goodwin, B. (2017). Critical thinking won't develop through osmosis. *Educational Leadership, 74*(5), 80–81.

Greater Good Magazine. (2019). Empathy quiz. https://greatergood.berkeley .edu/quizzes/take_quiz/empathy

Greer, J. L., Searby, L. J., & Thoma, S. J. (2015). Arrested development? Comparing educational leadership students with national norms on moral reasoning. *Educational Administration Quarterly, 51*(4), 511–542.

Grohol, J. (2018). Become a better listener: Active listening. Retrieved from https://psychcentral.com/lib/become-a-better-listener-active-listening/

Haiyan, Q., & Walker, A. (2014). Leading with empathy. In C. M. Branson & S. J. Gross (Eds.), *Handbook of ethical educational leadership*. New York: Routledge.

Hall, C. (2017). Police: Teacher steals homecoming money, spends it at casino. *Detroit Free Press*. https://www.freep.com/story/news/nation-now/2017/09/22/teacher-steals-homecoming-money/692200001/

Higginson, T. W. (1891, October.) "Emily Dickinson's letters." *The Atlantic*. Retrieved from https://www.theatlantic.com/magazine/archive/1891/10/emily-dickinsons-letters/306524/

Holte, K. L. (2009). *Shhhh!: A critical didactic relations analysis of the curriculum silentium; The hidden policy of silence regarding work related criticism from employees*. (Doctoral dissertation). University of Karlstad, Sweden.

Holte, K. L. (2014). The prevalence of silence. In C. M. Branson & S. J. Gross (Eds.), *Handbook of ethical educational leadership*. New York: Routledge.

Hsieh, T. (2010). Are you prepared for your next defining moment? *Harvard Business Review*.

Hull, J. (2018). The job of a school principal has changed a lot. Here's how we help them do it. Retrieved from https://educationpost.org/the-job-of-a-school-principal-has-changed-a-lot-heres-how-we-help-them-do-it/

Kellar, T. (2018). Teacher accused of stealing student's purse is superintendent's daughter. https://www.pennlive.com/news/2018/01/teacher_accused_of_stealing_st.html

Khalifa, M. (2018). *Culturally responsive school leadership*. Cambridge, MA: Harvard Education Press.

Maxwell, J. (2012). Are you really leading or just taking a walk? Retrieved from https://www.johnmaxwell.com/blog/are-you-really-leading-or-are-you-just-taking-a-walk/

McNae, R. (2014). Seeking social justice. In C. M. Branson & S. J. Gross (Eds.), *Handbook of ethical educational leadership*. New York: Routledge.

Meckler, L. (2018). Betsy DeVos panel rejects Obama-era effort to reduce discrimination in school discipline. Retrieved from https://www.washingtonpost.com/local/education/betsy-devos-school-safety-panel-takes-aim-at-obamas-discipline-guidance/2018/12/10/7e515700-f6b6-11e8-8c9a-860ce2a8148f_story.html?noredirect=on&utm_term=.e02a30234cec&wpisrc=nl_sb_smartbrief

MetLife. (2013). *The MetLife Survey of the American Teacher: Challenges for School Leadership*. https://www.metlife.com/content/dam/microsites/about/corporate-profile/MetLife-Teacher-Survey-2012.pdf

Murphy, J., Louis, K. S., & Smylie, M. (2017). Positive school leadership: How the Professional Standards for Educational Leaders can be brought to life. *Kappan, 99*(1), 21–24.

Murphy, J., & Smylie, M. A. (2016). What the new educational leadership standards really mean: The 2015 standards characterize leadership as intentional, strategic, and moral. *Principal Leadership, 16*(9), 34–37.

National Center for Education Statistics. (2018a). Children and youth with disabilities. https://nces.ed.gov/programs/coe/indicator_cgg.asp

National Center for Education Statistics. (2018b). Fast facts; Public school students eligible for free or reduced-price lunch. Retrieved from https://nces.ed.gov/fastfacts

National Center for Educational Statistics. (2018c). *Principal attrition and mobility: Results from the 2016–17 Principal Follow-up Survey.* https://nces.ed.gov/pubs2018/2018066.pdf

National Education Association. (2012). *The power of family school community partnerships: A training resource manual.* http://www2.nea.org/mediafiles/pdf/FSCP_Manual_2012.pdf

National Policy Board for Educational Administration (NPBEA). (2015). *Professional Standards for Educational Leaders.* Reston, VA: Author. https://www.wallacefoundation.org/knowledge-center/Documents/Professional-Standards-for-Educational-Leaders-2015.pdf

Nei, K., & Nei, D. (2018). Don't try to be the "fun boss"—and other lessons in ethical leadership. *Harvard Business Review.*

Nelson, S. W., & Guerra, P. L. (2014). Educator beliefs and cultural knowledge: Implications for school improvement efforts. *Educational Administration Quarterly, 50*(1), 67–95.

Newman, K. (2018). *How to make your workday more mindful.* https://greatergood.berkeley.edu/article/item/how_to_make_your_workday_more_mindful

Pew Research Center. (2018). The number of refugees admitted to the U.S. has fallen, especially among Muslims. Fact Tank: News in the Numbers (May 3). http://www.pewresearch.org/fact-tank/2018/05/03/the-number-of-refugees-admitted-to-the-u-s-has-fallen-especially-among-muslims/

Quaglia, R. J., & Corso, M. J. (2016). *Student voice.* Thousand Oaks, CA: Corwin.

Quaglia, R. J., Corso, M. J., Fox, K., & Dykes, G. (2017). *Aspire high: Imagining tomorrow's school today.* Thousand Oaks, CA: Corwin.

Robbins, M. (2018). How to bring your whole self to work. Retrieved from https://greatergood.berkeley.edu/article/item/how_to_bring_your_whole_self_to_work

Sacks, A. (2017). Empowering teachers to respond to change: With high levels of change expected, schools must set up structures that help teachers share their best thinking and manage change effectively. *Educational Leadership, 74*(9), 40–45.

Shapiro, J., & Stefkovich, J. (2016). *Multiple ethical paradigms.* New York: Routledge.

Shapiro, J. P. (2018). Foreword. In L. Bass, W. C. Frick, & M. D. Young (Eds.), *Developing ethical principles for school leadership.* New York: Routledge.

Sheninger, E. (2014). *Digital leadership: Changing paradigms for changing times.* Thousand Oaks, CA: Corwin.

Shields, (2014). Ethical leadership: A critical transformative approach. In C. M. Branson & S. J. Gross (Eds.), *Handbook of ethical educational leadership*. New York: Routledge.

Sianoja, M., Synek, C., de Bloom, J., Korpela, K., & Kinnunen, U. (2018). Enhancing daily well-being at work through lunchtime park walks and relaxation exercises: Recovery experiences as mediators. *Journal of Occupational Health Psychology, 23*(3), 428–442.

Singer, P. (1975). *Animal liberation: A new ethics for our treatment of animals.* New York: Random House.

Singleton, G. (2018). Beyond random acts of equity: Courageous conversations about transforming systemic culture. *The Learning Professional, 39*(5), 28–33.

Smith, D., Frey, N., Pumpian, I., & Fisher, D. (2017). *Building equity: Policies and practices to empower all learners.* Alexandra, VA: ASCD.

Spataro, S. E., & Bloch, J. (2018). "Can you repeat that?" Teaching active listening in management education. *Journal of Management Education, 42*(2), 168–198.

Starr, J. (2016). Lead with transparency and integrity. *Kappan, 98*(2), 72–73.

Starratt, J. (2014). The purpose of education. In C. M. Branson & S. J. Gross (Eds.), *Handbook of ethical educational leadership.* New York: Routledge.

Stefkovich, J. A. (2014). *Best interests of the students.* New York: Routledge.

Stoughton, S. (2016). Is the police-community relationship in America beyond repair? Retrieved from https://www.washingtonpost.com/opinions/is-the-police-community-relationship-in-america-beyond-repair/2016/07/08/595c638c-454b-11e6-bc99-7d269f8719b1_story.html?noredirect=on&utm_term=.74fef5c0295f

Terrell, R. D., & Lindsey, R. B. (2009). *Culturally proficient leadership: The personal journey begins within.* Thousand Oaks, CA: Corwin.

Toler, S. (2015). *Minute motivators for leaders.* Eugene, OR: Harvest House.

Tuana, N. (2014). An ethical leadership developmental framework. In C. M. Branson & S. J. Gross (Eds.), *Handbook of ethical educational leadership.* New York: Routledge.

Valcour, M. (2016). Steps to take when you're starting to feel burned out. *Harvard Business Review.*

Weger, H., Bell, G. C., Minei, E. M., & Robinson, M. C. (2014). The relative effectiveness of active listening in initial interactions. *International Journal of Listening, 28*(1), 13–31.

Wilson, J. D. (2017). Viewpoint. *Principal Leadership, 17*(5), 22–24.

Young, M. D., & Perrone, F. (2016). How are standards used, by whom, and to what end? *Journal of Research on Leadership Education, 11*(1), 3–11.

Zenger, J., & Folkman, J. (2016). What great listeners do. *Harvard Business Review.*

INDEX

Leadership That Makes an Impact

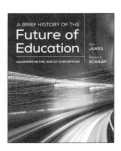

LYN SHARRATT

Explore 14 essential parameters to guide system and school leaders toward building powerful collaborative learning cultures.

MICHAEL FULLAN

How do you break the cycle of surface-level change to tackle complex challenges? *Nuance* is the answer.

IAN JUKES & RYAN L. SCHAAF

The digital environment has radically changed how students need to learn. Get ready to be challenged to accommodate today's learners.

ERIC SHENINGER

Lead for efficacy in these disruptive times! Cultivating school culture focused on the achievement of students while anticipating change is imperative.

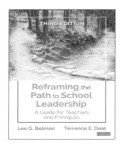

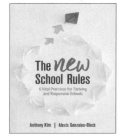

JOANNE MCEACHEN & MATTHEW KANE

Getting at the heart of what matters for students is key to deeper learning that connects with their lives.

LEE G. BOLMAN & TERRENCE E. DEAL

Sometimes all it takes to solve a problem is to reframe it by listening to wise advice from a trusted mentor.

PETER M. DEWITT

This go-to guide is written for coaches, leaders looking to be coached, and leaders interested in coaching burgeoning leaders.

ANTHONY KIM & ALEXIS GONZALES-BLACK

Designed to foster flexibility and continuous innovation, this resource expands cutting-edge management and organizational techniques to empower schools with the agility and responsiveness vital to their new environment.

To order your copies, visit **corwin.com/leadership**

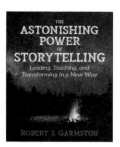

ROBERT J. GARMSTON

Stories have unique power to captivate and motivate action. This guidebook shows how to leverage storytelling to engage students.

JOYCE L. EPSTEIN

Strengthen programs of family and community engagement to promote equity and increase student success!

DEAN T. SPAULDING & GAIL M. SMITH

Help teams navigate the world of data analysis for ongoing school improvement with an easy-to-follow framework that dives deep into data-driven instruction.

KENNETH LEITHWOOD

By drawing on the numerous cases and stories, educators will gain a deep understanding of how to prepare the next wave of talented school leaders for success.

ANGELINE A. ANDERSON, SUSAN K. BORG, & STEPHANIE L. EDGAR

Centered on teacher voice and grounded in foundations of collaboration and data-informed planning, Transform Academy comes to life through its stories, and accompanying action steps.

AMY TEPPER & PATRICK FLYNN

Leaders know that feedback is essential to teacher development. This how-to guide helps leaders conduct comprehensive observations, analyze lessons, develop high-leverage action steps, and craft effective feedback.

MICHAEL FULLAN, JOANNE QUINN, & JOANNE MCEACHEN

This book defines what deep learning is, and takes up the question of how to mobilize complex whole-system change.

JOANNE QUINN, JOANNE MCEACHEN, MICHAEL FULLAN, MAG GARDNER, & MAX DRUMMY

This resource shows you how to design deep learning, measure progress, and assess the conditions to sustain innovation and mobilization.

A SAGE Publishing Company

Helping educators make the greatest impact

CORWIN HAS ONE MISSION: to enhance education through intentional professional learning.

We build long-term relationships with our authors, educators, clients, and associations who partner with us to develop and continuously improve the best evidence-based practices that establish and support lifelong learning.